One book that unites us all over the
that make us stop and wonder - if

WHY IS IT?

The Collection

Life is pure genius - it connects us to the world and puts an end to death.

Joan B. Foster

ISBN-10: 1985696673
ISBN-13: 978-1985696679

Published by Bell Publishing

Printed by CreateSpace, an Amazon.com company.
www.CreateSpace.com
Available from Amazon.com and other retail outlets.
Book design by Larry Smith
www.LarrySmithDesign.com

Please direct all inquiries to:
Bell Publishing at P.O. Box 44232, Fort Washington, MD 20749

Credits: Art Explosion

DEDICATION

To my good friend Cheryl who made me look at life through a totally different lens.

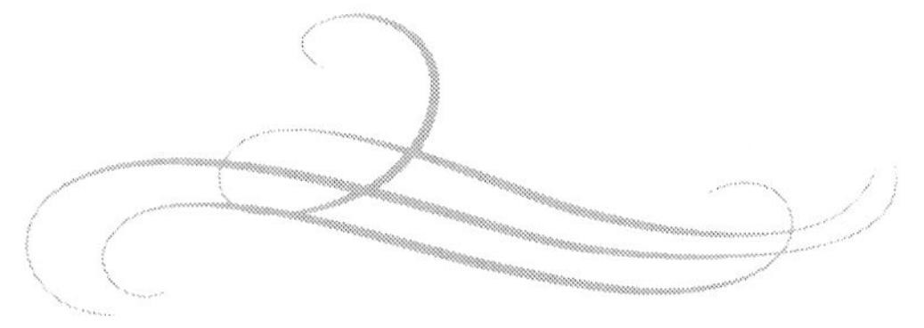

CONTENTS

ANIMALS **11**

KIDS **29**

LIFE **59**

POLITICS **128**

RELATIONSHIPS **149**

RELIGION **187**

SUCCESS **219**

TRANSITIONING **237**

OTHER **261**

INTRODUCTION

There is no end to the things that make us stop and wonder. Every day, questions about people or things pop up that we cannot comprehend. We have no clue as to why people do certain things or why we quickly shrug our shoulders and accept them. We make up things, create scenarios or dramatize imaginings for the sheer sake of entertainment. In fact, sometimes, the stories we dream up and fantasize about don't even sound right. Yet, millions of dollars are squandered each year at the movies or theater just for the sake of keeping us entertained.

We like talking out of the side of our mouths and making short talk, or cracking jokes, as they say, to our hearts content mostly because we like living on the edge. We repeat silly phrases because they snap us out of our reality and make us feel justified for living on the edge. We like our one liners because they are catchy, humorous, or shocking, and those things stick in our memories long after we have passed our better days. So when we need something to cheer us up, we can call them up and laugh to our hearts content.

Most of it is just stuff and nonsense – in other words, rubbish. But we like rubbish. It's like a person who insists on wearing a shaggy hairdo. Who wants to commit to a neatly trimmed haircut? Why do we put ourselves through it? It causes too much maintenance. If the hair is unruly, so what? No one would ever know when it's disheveled as long as they never see it neat and trimmed!

The random thoughts and ideas in this collection of ***Why Is It?*** thoughts are those kinds of phrases. They make us stop and wonder for a few moments – but then we continue with our lives. It does not matter whether any of it makes sense. Look. Life is hard enough for everyone, especially these days and most of us understand how important it is to have an outlet. The phrases here are intended to do just that.

The magic of enjoying life is simple. Some people look at it through a frosted glass believing that everything is cold, blurred, unclear and lonely -- they cannot connect with true experiences because they seem unreal. However, others stare in awe through a finely cut spherical, multi-faceted glass like lead crystal. It is through this finely cut glass that one sees artistic beauty and the wonders of the world. A treasure of true riches that cannot be compared.

So life is what we make of it. Sure, there will always be ups and downs. We can choose to swim up or downstream. However, no matter which way we go, it is comforting to know that we have the option of enjoying the ride whether on public or private transportation, with others or alone, with the radio on or in dead silence.

Life is a big show. It is pure genius! It is what connects us to the outside world; it is full of beautiful messages, opportunities, and grand episodes. Life is what puts an end to death. It is magic.

> “
>
> *There is no passion to be found playing small–in settling for a life that is less than the one you are capable of living.*
>
> Nelson Mandela

ANIMALS

Animals Have a Story, Too

“

The greatest day in your life and mine is when we take total responsibility for our attitudes. That's the day we truly grow up.

John C. Maxwell

— 1 —

Why is it dogs still love you even if they don't trust you?

— 2 —

Why is it the birds inform on cats, cat informs on dog but the dog doesn't give a flip?

— 3 —

Why is it road trips are heaven for a dog but hell for a cat?

— 4 —

How is it that a cat always lands on its feet but a dog crash lands?

— 5 —

If a turtle doesn't have a shell, is he homeless or naked?

— 6 —

If animals were not meant to be eaten, then why are they made out of meat?

— 7 —

Why is it no matter what you do, the cat always has the upper hand?

— 8 —

In horse racing, why do they award the rider and not the horse?

— 9 —

Until the lion has a storyteller, the hunter's stories will always be better.

— 10 —

Why is it people at the zoo are amazed to see a tiger eat 60 pounds of red meat at one sitting?

— 11 —

Why is it humans don't get to drop off their children at the pound?

— 12 —

What if pigs decided to slaughter humans?

— **13** —

Why is it we make our pets do tricks, parade them in front of a bunch of worthless judges and then we take the prize money?

— **14** —

Why is it we accuse people of behaving like animals when humans are more inhumane?

— **15** —

If dogs never pick their nose, why are they never crusty?

— **16** —

If dogs have a sixth sense, why do they keep hanging around their master?

— **17** —

If petting a dog lowers blood pressure, what does hugging a dog do?

— 18 —

Why is it smelly stuff is gross to human beings but divine to animals?

— 19 —

Why is it girls are 3 times more attracted to guys with a dog than a guy is to a girl with a dog?

— 20 —

Why is it perky eared dogs can hear better than floppy eared dogs?

— 21 —

Why is it smaller breeds live longer than larger breeds?

— 22 —

How is it a 5lb cat can chase away a 60lb dog?

— 23 —

If a 4oz blue bird can chase away an 8lb tom cat, why is it they are not used as body guards for the other little birds?

— 24 —

If African lions are the most social of all big cats, why is everyone so afraid of them?

— 25 —

If male lions can leap as far as 36 feet, why do we have them in open environments at the city zoo?

— 26 —

Why is it humans don't wise up like llamas and not overburden themselves with extra weight?

— 27 —

If parrots are so freakishly smart, then why don't they know when to be quiet?

— 28 —

Why is it dogs eat things like rocks, mud, disgusting dead animals, sticks and even stuff that might kill them?

— 29 —

Why is it dog owners living in tiny homes get a 100-pound pooping dog?

— 30 —

Why is it clutter doesn't bother kids as much as adults?

— 31 —

Why is it nobody brings soap or umbrella to a baby shower?

— 32 —

Why is it called hamburger but there's no ham in it?

— 33 —

Why is it dogs roll around in garbage or other smelly stuff?

— 34 —

What is it about a strutting chicken that make us laugh?

— 35 —

Why is it wool on the sheep doesn't shrink when it rains?

— 36 —

Why is it wishbones are supposed to be lucky?

— 37 —

Why is it stupid stuff animals do makes us laugh?

— 38 —

Why is it spiders give us the creeps?

ANIMALS

Part 2

Other Amazing Living Beings

— **1** —

Why can dogs train us a lot quicker than we can train them?

— **2** —

Why do they call it "getting your dog fixed" if afterwards it doesn't work anymore?

— **3** —

Why does the Easter bunny carry eggs? Rabbits don't lay eggs.

— **4** —

Why is it animals look like their masters?

— **5** —

Why is it dog lovers complain that cats are too independent?

— **6** —

Why is it dogs can understand you no matter what language you speak?

— 7 —

Why is it dogs hate cats unconditionally but love humans conditionally?

— 8 —

Why is it easier for dogs to train humans than for humans to train dogs?

— 9 —

Why is it people who own vicious dogs have to own them in pairs?

— 10 —

Why is it called duck sauce if there's no duck in it?

— 11 —

Why is it some folks think venomous snakes can be pets?

— 12 —

Why is it so hard to tame a porcupine?

ANIMALS

Part 3

Animal Rights

— 1 —

Why is it show animals make more than us?

— 2 —

Why is it snake owners think poisonous snakes can become pets?

— 3 —

Why is it so much easier to love dogs than people?

— 4 —

Why is it some people treat animals better than humans?

— 5 —

Why is it some people would rather spend all of their money on a stray animal than to give a couple of bucks to a homeless person?

— **6** —

Why is it that blowing in a dog's face makes it mad, yet when you take him on a car ride he sticks his head out the window?

— **7** —

Why is it we can spend millions of dollars researching trivia facts about animal life but cannot find enough money to feed, clothe and shelter the homeless?

— **8** —

Why is it we don't take a hint like the bears do and close shop in the winter?

— **9** —

Why is it we train animals to behave like humans but when they do, we get mad?

— 10 —

Why is it animals like sniffing humans too?

— 11 —

What is about dogs that makes man love them?

— 12 —

Why is it that a tiny baby can send a big dog packing?

KIDS

Life's Little Munchkins

"

Life is not a problem to be solved, but a reality to be experienced.

Soren Kierkegaard

— **1** —

How is it that kids who we think are too young, actually understand everything we're saying?

— **2** —

If it's such a humanitarian thing to do, why is adoption so expensive?

— **3** —

If parents say, "Never take candy from strangers", why celebrate Halloween?

— **4** —

If peanut butter cookies are made from peanut butter, then what are Girl Scout cookies made out of?

— **5** —

In that song, 'she'll be coming around the mountain', who is SHE?

— **6** —

Why do parents encourage kids to play with explosives on Independence Day?

— **7** —

Why do Moms think the most important about having an accident is whether or not your underwear is clean?

— **8** —

Why is it parents force their children to say thanks for something they don't want?

— **9** —

Why do people drop babies off on the church's doorstep?

— **10** —

Why do folk think it's easy for a woman to raise 5-6 kids alone but a man only needs to "help"?

— 11 —

Why are sex ed movies but not Bible stories allowed in school?

— 12 —

Why does the word "nap" tends to make babies cry?

— 13 —

Where in the nursery rhyme does it say humpty dumpty is an egg?

— 14 —

Why is it so many people have to go way overseas to find a kid they can adopt?

— 15 —

Why aren't marbles made out of marble instead of glass, clay, or other materials?

— 16 —

Why do all babies look alike no matter what?

— 17 —

Why do black babies look white when they are born?

— 18 —

Why do mothers always cry when they punish a child?

— 19 —

Why do parents give kids options for doing something and then get angry with the kids when they choose the "wrong" one?

— 20 —

Why do parents think beating the crap out of their children will stop them from fighting?

— 21 —

Why does Donald Duck wear a towel when he comes out of the shower, when he doesn't usually wear any pants?

— 22 —

Why does Goofy stand on two legs when Pluto remains on four? They're both dogs.

— 23 —

Why does honey come in plastic bears and not plastic bees?

— 24 —

Why does the Easter bunny carry eggs? Rabbits don't lay eggs.

— 25 —

Why doesn't McDonald's sell hot dogs?

— 26 —

Why is it we think telling a kid to stop "acting like a child" is a good thing to do?

— 27 —

Why is it a baby's illness is harder on adults than the baby?

— **28** —

Why is it adults think little children cannot hear or understand adult body language.

— **29** —

Why is it America, home of the brave, has so many children on the waiting list to be adopted?

— **30** —

Why is it an only child can be one parent's pride but the other's nightmare?

— **31** —

Why is it babies smile when they pass gas?

— **32** —

Why is it children are not involved in recognizing and rewarding teachers?

— 33 —

Why is it kids like sticking things up their nose?

— 34 —

Why is it kids like flushing stuff down the toilet?

— 35 —

Why is it that despite warning, parents do dumb stuff to their kids like giving them bad boy names, letting pedophiles babysit them, or getting them hooked on junk food?

— 36 —

Why is it that we think it's funny to watch kids do bizarre things?

— 37 —

Why is it necessary to discipline children or set foundations for good behavior if we're just going to let them do anything they want, anyway?

— 38 —

Why is it that blue is for boys and pink for girls?

— 39 —

Why is it some kids cannot go to sleep until you take them for a drive in the car?

— 40 —

Why is it the least likely kid makes the biggest bully?

KIDS

Part 2

We're All Just Kids in Big Pants

— **1** —

Why is it children can't hear and watch TV at the same time?

— **2** —

Why is it children think their parents never want them to leave home?

— **3** —

Why is it children keep returning home even after marriage?

— **4** —

Why is it fast food places keep getting slower and slower?

— **5** —

Why is it Grandparents let their grandchildren get away with things they didn't allow their own children to get away with?

— 6 —

Why is it if the teenager likes it, Moms do not and if Mom's like it, kids don't?

— 7 —

Why is it kids always want more than you can possibly give?

— 8 —

Why is it kids don't need you until you're on the phone?

— 9 —

Why is it large families have absolutely no respect for your sofa?

— 10 —

Why is it little kids can look so innocent but be so bad?

— 11 —

Why is it only maternal grandparents can do no wrong in their grandchildren's eyes?

— **12** —

Why is it more kids are going to psychotherapists these days?

— **13** —

Why is it most school buses don't have seat belts?

— **14** —

Why is it no matter how much scolding we get from the maternal grandparents, we still feel loved?

— **15** —

Why is it no one wants to be a grandparent anymore?

— **16** —

Why is it nursery rhymes and bedtime stories are so violent?

— **17** —

Why is it ordinary people end up with the most extraordinary children?

— 18 —

Why is it our Mother's cooking tastes better than anybody else's even though we hated it while growing up?

— 19 —

Why is it parents give advice even when they know nothing about the subject?

— 20 —

Why is it parents apologize for punishing their children?

— 21 —

Why is it parents can't punish kids without punishing themselves?

— 22 —

Why is it parents constantly worry about protecting their children from external influences, yet they bring guns and alcohol into the house?

— 23 —

Why is it parents make kids to say thanks for something they do not want?

— 24 —

Why is it parents who are their child's best friend complain when the kid disobey them?

— 25 —

Why do people base credit worthiness off gross income but child support off their net?

— 26 —

Why is it people know where to get their kids' $200 sneakers, but don't where their next meal is coming from?

— 27 —

Why is it people try to get cats to act like dogs?

— 28 —

Why is it so hard for minister's children to turn out well?

— 29 —

Why is it grandmothers don't like to babysit anymore?

— 30 —

Why is it so important to annotate baby's "first time"?

— 31 —

Why is it that only adults have difficulty with childproof bottles?

— 32 —

Why is it that our children can't read a Bible in school, but they can in prison?

— 33 —

Why is it kids have all the energy?

— 34 —

Why is it the more you hang around kids, the younger you act?

— 35 —

Why is it the more kids you have to care for, the more settled minded you become?

— 36 —

Why is it kids never seem to get tired?

— 37 —

Why is it kids like spinning around 10 times until they get dizzy enough to fall down?

— 38 —

Why is it millennials don't want kids?

— 39 —

Why is it kids hate to go to bed?

— 40 —

Why is it parents give their kids constant activity tablets?

— 41 —

Why is it we always tell kids to grow up but hate it when they do?

— 40 —

Why is it modern parenting is so crazy?

— 41 —

Why is it parents don't know the kids are spoiled until it's too late?

Part 3

When in Doubt, Choose Kids

— 1 —

Why is it that people say they "slept like a baby" when babies wake up, like, every two hours?

— 2 —

Why is it there are a zillion pictures of the first baby but only one snapshot of the second one?

— 3 —

Why is it the very people who protest abortion won't adopt children?

— 4 —

Why is it the very child that needs to be in school is always out?

— 5 —

Why is it the least deserving child always wants more?

— **6** —

Why is it we grow up and forget what it was like to be a kid?

— **7** —

Why is it the first child's baby book highlights all of the firsts, (i.e., her first burp, his first smile), but in the second child's baby book, there's nothing?

— **8** —

Why is it that adults with multiple personalities are put in a mental hospitals, but a child with imaginary friends is "cute"?

— **9** —

Why is it we think our kids are the perfect ones?

— **10** —

Why is it we are better at remembering what we didn't get than what we did get for Christmas?

— 11 —

Why is it we can get funding to teach children safe sex but not humanitarianism?

— 12 —

Why is it we cry when people leave this world but laugh when a baby comes to this world?

— 13 —

Why is it we feel more comfortable with our maternal grandparents?

— 14 —

Why is it we had 9 months to plan but are still flustered when the baby comes?

— 15 —

Why is it we put junk food in the house and then tell the kids not to eat it?

— 16 —

Why is it when a boy "stops acting like a child" and starts acting like a man, parents get upset?

— 17 —

Why is it when you like it, your teenager doesn't?

— 18 —

Why is it when going on a road trip or something, kids don't need to use the bathroom until you get on the road?

— 19 —

Why is it you don't notice a child's growth spurt until you haven't seen him for several days?

— 20 —

Why is it you don't realize how old you are until you interact with a teenager?

— 21 —

Why is it you have to drag the kids off to summer camp and then you have to drag them back home?

— 22 —

Why is it you never know how much patience you have until you have children?

— 23 —

Why is it parents always expect teachers to go over and beyond the call of duty for their child but the parent is never available for consultation?

— 24 —

How come you don't know until you grow up that this crap isn't what you expected?

— 25 —

Who would have thought that becoming an adult would be the dumbest thing you ever did?

— 26 —

How can you really know something unless you put it in your mouth?

— 27 —

Why is it babies wait until the quiet wee hours of the night to start crying for no reason?

— 28 —

Why is it no stick men are fat?

— 29 —

Why is it everything's fine until a kid gets cozy in bed then for some reason, they pee?

— 30 —

Why do we insist on putting huge stuffed Teddy Bears and talking animals in our kid's faces?

— 31 —

How is it that a child can ask questions that a wise man cannot answer?

— 32 —

Why is it that no matter how much you scrub them, children are always manage to find some way to be sticky?

— 33 —

Why is it kids lie right to your face about stuff that is obviously a lie?

— 34 —

Why is it people don't want kids to mark up the walls but they can mark up their bodies?

— **35** —

Why is it they can't eat just one chip and neither can we?

— **36** —

Why is it after 12 years of school, we only retain 10%, then use only 10% of that?

— **37** —

Why is it kids can spot an appeasement gift quicker than an adult?

— **38** —

Why is it more time is spent encouraging kids to get closer to an individually owned tablet than to a family dinner table?

— **39** —

Why is it so hard for adults to see through the freshness of a kid's eyes?

LIFE

Life's Little Ironies

— 1 —

A clever man wants to change the world; but a wise one wants to change himself.

— 2 —

Funny how the solutions to stress can be so stressful!

— 3 —

Get a life; somebody's waiting for you to wake up.

— 4 —

Good thing about pessimists is they never expect good returns; so borrow from them.

— 5 —

Why do we say that guilty people don't seem to have a conscience?

— 6 —

Having real freedom is having no bondages – not even money.

— 7 —

Horse sense is the thing a horse has which keeps it from betting on people.

— 8 —

How can a massage be considered good if it's really "bad"?

— 9 —

How come some people put so much significance on life they can't enjoy it?

— 10 —

How come the more education some people have, the less common sense?

— 11 —

If opposites attract, why don't Blacks and Whites?

— 12 —

If our body temperature is normally 98.6 degrees, how come when it's 98 degrees outside, no one is comfortable?

— 13 —

If someone with multiple personalities threatens to kill himself, is it considered a hostage situation?

— 14 —

If you're a kleptomaniac, is there something you can take for it?

— 15 —

If the funeral procession is at night, do folks drive with their lights off?

— 16 —

In court, why do they ask if you swear to tell the truth? If you're planning on lying, do they really think you'll tell them so?

— **17** —

Introverts communicate by not communicating?

— **18** —

Is it true – the smaller the family, the larger the house?

— **19** —

Isn't it a bit unnerving that doctors call what they do "practice"?

— **20** —

It doesn't matter what temperature a room is, it's always room temperature.

— **21** —

Why is it impossible to unchain fools from their folly?

— **22** —

Why is it easier to enjoy rules made for someone else?

— 23 —

Why is it lips turned up bring happiness to anyone, but lips turned down runs people away?

— 24 —

Why is it little people tend to have such big personalities?

— 25 —

Money will not buy happiness, but at least it will let you be unhappy in nice places.

— 26 —

Most people react first, then act?

— 27 —

Never underestimate the power of very stupid people in large groups.

— 28 —

Why is it outsiders see us better for who we are than our family?

— 29 —

Why is it people don't change; they just become more like themselves as they get older?

— 30 —

Why do people fight over stuff they don't care about?

— 31 —

Why is it people like holding onto the past?

— 32 —

Why is it people make appointments they have no intention of keeping?

— 33 —

Why is it people tend to like you after you're dead?

— 34 —

Why is it people think everything amounts to how they feel?

— **35** —

Why do shopping centers always go down when larger chain stores leave?

— **36** —

Shouldn't women earn bachelorette's instead of bachelor degrees?

— **37** —

Why is it simple stuff gets so complicated when smart people get involved?

— **38** —

Why is it the bride always pays for the wedding?

— **39** —

True love doesn't have a happy ending because true love never ends.

— **40** —

We find out how strong we are when we go through something.

— **41** —

What makes doctors think patients don't want to know what's going on with their bodies?

— **42** —

What would happen if there were no hypothetical questions?

— **43** —

When we're hungry and broke we eat foods we don't even like.

— **44** —

Ordinarily, ideas come from nowhere except when you're desperate.

— **45** —

Who do people repeat the same old story even if you say you heard it already?

— **46** —

Why is it nobody over 40 wants to claim their age in spite of all they've been through?

— **47** —

Why is it older people feel they've got license to say whatever pops into their heads?

— **48** —

Why is it the older some people get, the younger they act?

— **49** —

Why is it old age creeps up on you so fast?

— **50** —

Why is it nose and body piercings freak out some people?

— 51 —

Why are builders afraid to have a 13th floor but book publishers aren't afraid to have a Chapter 11?

— 52 —

Why are hurricanes named after women?

— 53 —

Why are rat traps in the car-care section of my supermarket?

— 54 —

Why are the nicknames we most hate are the ones best remembered?

— 55 —

Why are there seeds in seeded grapes, but no bones in a boned fillet?

— 56 —

Why are they called stairs inside but called steps when they are outside?

— 57 —

Why can't we be wise enough to walk away from foolishness?

— 58 —

Why can't we work on the weekend and be off during the week?

— 59 —

Why complain about having a dress code if secretly everyone admits "everybody else" needs it?

— 60 —

Why do banks charge you an 'insufficient funds' fee for money they already know you don't have?

— 61 —

Why do servers give overweight people larger portions than thinner people?

— 62 —

Why do employees code 8 hour days if statistics show they only work 65% of the day or less?

— 63 —

Why do four passenger cars have only two airbags instead of four?

— 64 —

Why do mechanics always drive ratty cars?

— 65 —

Why do models have to be sizes 5-6 but the majority of women in the world are 12-16s?

— 66 —

Why do most businesses honor the dress code until a sexy woman breaks it?

— 67 —

Why do other people think they need to keep you grounded?

— 68 —

Why do people let you take the blame but won't give you the credit?

— 69 —

Why do people skip breakfast more even though this is when the stomach is emptiest?

— 70 —

Why do people worry about becoming perfect when they know it's impossible?

— 71 —

Why do slow people try to drag down fast people?

— 72 —

Why do some people see the whole world as a garden; others see a jungle?

— 73 —

Why do they insist you make an appointment if you're still going to have to wait before you see the doctor ?

— 74 —

Why do they never have your size during the sale?

— 75 —

Why do they put Braille on the number pads of drive-through bank machines?

— 76 —

Why do they sterilize needles for lethal injections?

— 77 —

Why is it mistakes are touted as stepping stones to success but we're warned against them?

— 78 —

Why is it violent movies are used to teach what we should not do?

— 79 —

Why do we serve so many different dishes on Thanksgiving?

— 80 —

Why do white women always fall down when they're being chased?

— 81 —

Why is it people get upset when their advice isn't taken?

— 82 —

Why is it all the "good" movies are about sex, violence and negative images?

— 83 —

Why is it all the row houses in the city look alike?

— 84 —

Why is it anorexia is more rampant among the rich?

— 85 —

Why is it bad things come in threes?

— 86 —

Why is it birds don't poop on the car until right after you wax it?

— 87 —

Why is it cars with exhaust problems always pull in front of you at the traffic light and then rev the engine?

— 88 —

Why is it casual day is interpreted a million different ways?

— 89 —

Why is it company policy never changes until the rules are broken by someone on the board?

— 90 —

Why is it cops take such pleasure in stopping and detaining speeders?

— 91 —

Why is it dentists get mad if you don't do what they tell you?

— 92 —

Why is it dentists start grilling you as soon as they start drilling your mouth?

— 93 —

Why is it doctors don't speak in layman's terms so people can understand what the heck's going on?

— 94 —

Why is it doctors have to practice at making their handwriting illegible?

— 95 —

Why is it driver's education lasts only a few weeks but it takes years to learn how to drive?

— 96 —

Why is it easier to fall asleep behind the wheel?

— 97 —

Why is it easier to smile at a perfect stranger than someone we know?

— 98 —

Why is it easy to criticize but hard to recognize value?

— 99 —

Why is it everybody feels they can advise pregnant women?

— 100 —

Why is it everybody gets mad with older people for dressing young?

— 101 —

Why is it everybody tries to go on vacation at the same time?

— 102 —

Why is it everybody wants to live forever? For what?

— 103 —

Why is it everybody wants to put up the Christmas tree but nobody wants to take it down?

— 104 —

Why is it everybody works so hard to do well at jobs they hate?

— 105 —

Why is it everybody's suing somebody?

— 106 —

Why is it everybody's trying to have their own business?

— 107 —

Why is it everyone's in such a rush to go somewhere and get stressed out?

— 108 —

Why is it everything falls apart when the Mother leaves?

— 109 —

Why is it easier to help a stranger than family?

— 110 —

Why is it considered wise to have wisdom teeth removed?

— 111 —

Is math really that important anymore?

— 112 —

Why is it we have to work?

— 113 —

Why is it easier to get angry than to show love if emotion is just emotion?

— 114 —

Why is it parents of defiant or aggressive kids wait too late to accept advice?

— 115 —

Why is it parents spoil one kid but not the other?

— 116 —

Why is it all the weird stuff happens at 3 a.m.?

— 117 —

Why is it you get sleepy while sitting in the sun?

— 118 —

Why is it somebody breathing down your neck in the dark makes your skin crawl?

— 119 —

Why is it stuff's funniest when it's something you're not supposed to laugh about?

— 120 —

Why is it that as soon as you get your computer figured out, it's time for a new one?

— 121 —

Why is it so easy to accumulate useless stuff but hard to get rid of it?

— 122 —

Why is it some people work too hard and others hardly work?

"

Too often we underestimate the power of a touch, a smile, a kind word, a listening ear, an honest compliment, or the smallest act of caring, all of which have the potential to turn a life around.

Leo Buscaglia

LIFE

Part 2

Don't Blink or You'll Miss It

— 1 —

Why is it families spread far apart and then complain about never seeing each other?

— 2 —

Why is it forced laughter is different from spontaneous laughter but the result is the same?

— 3 —

Why is it friends think they can surprise you on your birthday?

— 4 —

Why is it greedy people are stingy and stingy people are greedy?

— 5 —

Why is it house painting is easy until you get started?

— 6 —

If truth is the most valuable thing we have, why don't we value it?

— 7 —

Why is it insurance is so costly when insurance is one of the biggest money making industries?

— 8 —

Why is it mean and rough people seem to live longer?

— 9 —

Why is it misery loves company?

— 10 —

Why is it there are so many Cesarean births these days?

— 11 —

Why is it Mothers teach the girls independence but teach the boys laziness?

— 12 —

Why is it they replay horrifying race track accidents to the crowd?

— 13 —

Why is it newly developed products cost so much?

— 14 —

Why is it news reporters ask the dumbest questions during tragic events like, "Would you do it again?"

— 15 —

Why is it no matter how well you plan Thanksgiving dinner, something will be cold?

— 16 —

Why is it no matter what you do, you still end up running to catch your flight?

— **17** —

Why is it no one wants to destroy bridges even if they're dangerous ?

— **18** —

Why is it old people are afraid to go to the hospital?

— **19** —

Why is it optometrists dilate your pupils until you can't see and then tell you to read?

— **20** —

Why is it some panty hose manufacturers still think a woman's crotch is halfway her thighs?

— **21** —

Why is it people always want something they can't handle?

— 22 —

Why is it people won't try on your prosthesis but will try on your eyeglasses?

— 23 —

Why is it people take chances yelling or shaking fists at folk in traffic?

— 24 —

Why is it people are so quick to comment about overweight people's diets and health?

— 25 —

Why is it people blame others when they discover the secret they confided is no longer a secret?

— 26 —

Why is it people bottle up anxieties all year long only to get depressed at year end?

— 27 —

Why is it Northerners think they're better than Southerners?

— 28 —

Why is it people get paid big bucks to pretend they're someone else?

— 29 —

Why is it people hold their anger in until they're ready to explode?

— 30 —

Why is it people keep asking you if you're asleep until you wake up?

— 31 —

Why is it people lie at funerals about the deceased's conduct?

— 32 —

Why is it people over 40 feel compelled to explain why they have issues?

— **33** —

Why is it people think if they can't smell the alcohol on their breath, you can't smell it either?

— **34** —

Why is it people think living is easier than dying?

— **35** —

How can folk who don't understand English pass the written driver's license test quicker than average Americans?

— **36** —

Why is it greedy folk are shocked when scammed?

— **37** —

Why is it people who hate doing laundry buy so many clothes?

— **38** —

Why is it folk living in mud slide potential zones keep re-building?

— **39** —

Why is it people who love to eat love to cook?

— **40** —

Why is it those who need money the most cannot borrow but those who don't have no problem?

— **41** —

Why is it hardworking folk feel guilty for taking a break?

— **42** —

Why is it people without credit can't get any?

— 43 —

Why is it people won't give to charity unless there's something in it for them like a tax write off?

— 44 —

If everybody wants to stamp it out, why is it still around?

— 45 —

Why is it protesters talk about saving lives but not about preserving hope?

— 46 —

Why is it resident aliens get treated better than residents?

— 47 —

Why is it smokers want the right to smoke around who don't smoke?

— 48 —

Why is it so hard for people to live and let live?

— 49 —

Why is it so easy to be angry if anger takes so much more energy than any other emotion?

— 50 —

Why is it so hard for smart people to understand simple things?

— 51 —

Why is it so hard to exercise alone?

— 52 —

Why is it so hard to find time to write letters these days?

— 53 —

Why is it so hard to forgive and forget?

— 54 —

Why is it so hard to forgive people who make innocent mistakes?

— 55 —

Why is it so hard to see elderly citizens behind the wheel of their car?

— 56 —

Why is it so hard to tell somebody how you really feel until you've "had it"?

— 57 —

Why is it so much fun to eat breakfast foods later in the day?

— 58 —

Why is it some people never think it's their fault?

— 59 —

Why is it some people put more energy into being depressed than happy?

— 60 —

Why is it some people will swerve to avoid hitting an animal only to kill a human being?

— 61 —

Why is it some folk keep hanging around with chickens yet say they want to fly and soar like the eagles?

— 62 —

Why is it some people always ask for advice but don't ever take it?

— 63 —

Why is it some people always want favor but never return it?

— 64 —

Why is it some people are perfectly content to let life happen to them?

— 65 —

Why is it some people borrow so much they make you think they're making a full-time career of it?

— 66 —

Why is it some people couldn't keep a secret if their life depended on it?

— 67 —

Why is it some people don't know the meaning of the word "NO"?

— 68 —

Why is it some people know more about your business than theirs?

— 69 —

Why is it some people stay in the same corner of the world and never realize there's much more to life?

— 70 —

Why is it some people take chances at not having insurance?

— 71 —

Why is it some people will do anything for money?

— **72** —

Why is it some women can't find anything pleasant to say about another woman?

— **73** —

Why is it only something drastic can make a man admit he's an alcoholic?

— **74** —

Why is it that as long as everything is going along smoothly, we hear nothing about the state of the economy?

— **75** —

Why is it that everybody thinks overweight people are supposed to be jolly?

— **76** —

Why is it that outspoken White women are considered assertive; but Black women are considered aggressive?

— **77** —

Why is it easier to believe there's a billions of stars in the sky than to believe a wet paint sign?

— **78** —

Why is it that the more appliances and more modern conveniences we have, the lazier we get?

— **79** —

Why is it that rather than bettering themselves, some folk waste time criticizing others?

— **80** —

Why is it people worry about tomorrow but have no confidence in today?

— **81** —

Why is it the ambulance takes forever to get you to the hospital?

— 82 —

Why is it the bank never tells you how much money they earned off your money?

— 83 —

Why is it the car you want always costs more?

— 84 —

Why is it the computer goes down just before you save?

— 85 —

Why is it the doctor can make you wait forever to see him, but he can't wait for his bill to be paid?

— 86 —

Why is it the doctor gets all the credit for the work the nurses do?

— 87 —

Why is it the doctor makes you wait forever then only spends seconds with you?

— 88 —

Why is it the doctor thinks he knows more about our body than we do?

— 89 —

Why is it the express lines always take longer?

— 90 —

Why is it the instructor always calls on you when you don’t know the answer?

— 91 —

Why is it the insurance company never gives back your money even if you never had a wreck?

— **92** —

Why is it Ladies Rooms have lounges but not the Mens Room?

— **93** —

Why is it the larger the family, the smaller the house?

— **94** —

Why is it the meaner the person, the longer the life?

— **95** —

Why is it the more food you buy, the more you consume?

— **96** —

Why is it the more good news people receive, the more confused they get?

— **97** —

Why is it the more we think and talk about it, the worse a situation gets?

— **98** —

Why is it the more you give someone, the more they want and demand?

— **99** —

Why is it the overnight deposit at the ATM machine is maintained by someone other than the bank?

— **100** —

Why is it the people in D.C., the Nation's capitol, have to foot the bill for commuters?

— **101** —

Why is it the people who always crack on you can never take a joke?

— **102** —

Why is it the people who do not have a life manage to paint such a colorful picture of yours?

— 103 —

Why is it folk who insist that "age is just a number", either lie or clam up when asked their's?

— 104 —

Why is it the people whose birthdays you can't remember always remember your birthday and your family's, too?

— 105 —

Why is it the person gets back from the trip before you get the post card?

— 106 —

Why is it a person whose life is in shambles likes advising others?

— 107 —

Why is it the police cars come out of nowhere when a silent alarm is triggered?

— 108 —

Why is it the ratings of the news reporting depend on negativity?

— 109 —

Why is it the richer we become, the less we have to give to charity?

— 110 —

Why is it the subway escalators always break when you're carrying an extra load?

— 111 —

Why is it we call it an egg roll?

— 112 —

Why is it stuff is cheaper online compared to in the stores?

— 113 —

Why is it we overvalue stuff?

LIFE

Part 3

The Mysteries of Life

— 1 —

Why is it the term "adoption service" sounds self serving?

— 2 —

Why is it the truly gifted teachers get less reward and recognition than the "money grubbers"?

— 3 —

Why is it uninvited guests wear out their welcome faster than the hostess' patience?

— 4 —

Why is it the utility bills always increase, even if you go on vacation and board up the house for the winter?

— 5 —

Why is it there's only one bank teller when you're in a hurry?

— 6 —

Why is it today's cashiers can't count back change?

— 7 —

Why is it tornado and hurricane regions are full of trailers and mobile homes?

— 8 —

Why is it tourists think everybody they walk past knows the directions to their next tourist stop?

— 9 —

Why is it traffic always gets backed up when you have an important appointment that you absolutely cannot miss?

— 10 —

Why is it ugly people have so much to say about how other people look?

— 11 —

Why is it we complain about the problem, but never have any solutions?

— 12 —

Why is it we always know how much we need to borrow but can't remember how much we have to pay back?

— 13 —

Why is it we always take our anger out on someone else instead of the person that made us mad?

— 14 —

Why is it we can eat a variety of foods separately but get sick when we mix them?

— 15 —

Why is it we can never find anything even though computers do the filing?

— 16 —

Why is it sloppy folk have the nerve to criticize other people's homes?

— 17 —

Why is it we don't call it "weekstart" instead of "weekend"?

— 18 —

Why is it we don't care about our age until we see gray hair and wrinkles?

— 19 —

Why is it we don't know how much peace we've had until it's gone?

— 20 —

Why is it we don't know what good entertainment or journalism is anymore?

— 21 —

Why is it we don't mind stereotyping unless it involves us?

— 22 —

Why is it we expect so much more out of others that we do ourselves?

— 23 —

Why is it we feel good about our ideas until we hear somebody else's?

— 24 —

Why is it we feel it necessary to explain our odd behavior to perfect strangers?

— 25 —

Why is it we focus more on the negative forces in society?

— 26 —

Why is it we get real serious about life when we come back from visiting another country?

— **27** —

Why is it after 12 years of school, we only retain 10%, then use only 10% of that?

— **28** —

Why is it we grow up to be just like the person we don't want to become?

— **29** —

Why is it we have not figured out that it is not necessary to react to everything?

— **30** —

Why is it we have to plan to take time for ourselves?

— **31** —

Why is it we have to walk to our cars instead of making our cars come to us?

— 32 —

Why is it we keep automating and trying to improve everything that is already perfect?

— 33 —

Why is it we keep buying cheap, flimsy cup holders that don't work?

— 34 —

Why is it we keep giving our money to Uncle Sam like he's part of the family?

— 35 —

Why is it we keep saying the customer's always right even when they're wrong?

— 36 —

Why is it we keep trying to make everything equal?

— 37 —

Why is it we know and get along better with people at work than our own family?

— 38 —

Why is it we let hairdressers with awful haircuts do our hair?

— 39 —

Why is it we let the bank get away with giving us our money only when they're good and ready?

— 40 —

Why is it we look worse in a photo than in real life?

— 41 —

Why is it we mimic people with thick accents while we're talking to them?

— 42 —

Why is it we never predict what we think is going to happen but after something happens, we claim we knew beforehand?

— 43 —

Why is it we often admire softer spoken people but often run all over them anyway?

— 44 —

Why is it we pay lawyers to scam us?

— 45 —

Why is it we prejudge people although the law says a man is supposed to be innocent until proven guilty?

— 46 —

Why is it we punish people for telling the truth if it's so important?

— **47** —

Why is it we put off for tomorrow what we should do today and we do today what should wait until tomorrow?

— **48** —

How can someone can give more than 100%?

— **49** —

Why is it we still don't have enough time to get everything done?

— **50** —

Why is it we study subjects in school that we have no use for later?

— **51** —

Why is it we tend to trust people who wear glasses?

— **52** —

Why is it we think it's funny when someone gets tripped up?

— **53** —

Why is it we think we are so important?

— **54** —

Why is it we'd rather take advice from the person who has credentials but no experience over the person with the experience?

— **55** —

Why is it we're always shocked when older people curse and act ugly?

— **56** —

Why is it we're paying someone else fees when they ought to be paying us?

— **57** —

Why is it we're such harsh judges and critics until we fall into the same situation?

— **58** —

Why is it when people do something nice for somebody they have to tell the whole world about it?

— **59** —

Why is it when they throw you a surprise party, the timing is lousy and you don't want it?

— **60** —

Why is it when we find out we can't have something, we want it even more?

— **61** —

Why is it when we tell somebody not to try something, they do it anyway?

— **62** —

Why is it when you ask for a Sprite they bring a 7-Up and when you ask for a Coke they bring you a Pepsi?

— 63 —

Why is it when you go to the dentist your teeth always need some work?

— 64 —

Why is it when you need a good listening ear, everybody has something else to do?

— 65 —

Why is it when you meet someone who remembers you, you pretend to remember them?

— 66 —

Why is it when you take off sick from work, people call you anyway?

— 67 —

Why is it when you take the car in to repair one thing they repair something else?

— 68 —

Why is it when you tell someone you don't want to talk about it, they bug you?

— 69 —

Why is it when you're looking bad, you run into people that know you, but when you're looking good, you don't see anybody that knows you?

— 70 —

Why is it when your car gets stolen, it never comes back with enough damage to convince the insurance company to get you a new one?

— 71 —

Why is it when your order comes back wrong a couple of times, you feel guilty about complaining about it?

— **72** —

Why is it women's clothes cost more?

— **73** —

Why is it women's dry cleaning costs more?

— **74** —

Why is it you can fly around the country quicker than you can check your baggage?

— **75** —

Why is it you can never figure out which junk mail to throw out?

— **76** —

Why is it you can never find a gas station when you're about to run out of gas?

— **77** —

Why is it you can never find a room when you're dead tired?

— 78 —

Why is it you can never find what you're looking for until you stop looking?

— 79 —

Why is it you cannot remember what you were getting ready to do until you retrace your steps?

— 80 —

Why is it you don't realize somebody's been making a living off of you until you lose your apartment?

— 81 —

Why is it you don't see each other until there's a death in the family?

— 82 —

Why is it you don't speak to your neighbor all year until Christmas?

— 83 —

Why is it you either greatly respect or totally disrespect a policeman's uniform?

— 84 —

Why is it you feel OK until somebody says you look bad?

— 85 —

Why is it you come back from the with everything else except what you went to the store to get?

— 86 —

Why is it you have to be wary of people who say "I promise" all the time?

— 87 —

Why is it you have to keep reminding professional, very bright people, when they're in violation of dress codes?

— 88 —

Why is it you have to repeat the order so many times?

— 89 —

Why is it you have to take a deep breath and count to 10 when you're upset?

— 90 —

Why is it you have to yell at the drive-through cashier?

— 91 —

Why is it you look OK in your lighting at home but in the lighting everywhere else you look awful?

— 92 —

Why is it you never know how happy you are until you get a look at the other guy's life?

— 93 —

Why is it you never need something until you throw it out?

— 94 —

Why is it you stay on hold forever waiting for personalized service; but as soon as you have to put the receiver on hold for a second, they come and hang up on you?

— 95 —

Why is it your friends think the best way to help you with your problems is to talk about theirs?

— 96 —

Why is it your neighbor keeps the music up on maximum volume but all you can hear is the bass?

— 97 —

Why is it your optical lenses never feel right when you first get them?

— 98 —

Why is it your stomach waits until it gets quiet before it growls?

— 99 —

Why is it, for some reason, you keep trying to give hints to clueless people?

— 100 —

Why is it, if everybody's created equal, are some people broke?

— 101 —

Why is it, no matter how hard you try, there are some people who you simply cannot help?

— 102 —

Why is it, regardless of how well a leader performs, people who grew up with him will not follow him?

— 103 —

Why is it, without going through trial and error, Black people figured out cobras, rattlers, pythons and other snakes cannot be domesticated?

— 104 —

Why is there always at least one person in the crowd who couldn't care less?

— 105 —

Why isn't technology progressing in gynecology as in other medical fields so it isn't necessary for the GYN to physically examine women?

— 106 —

Why it is the Secret Service can't keep a secret?

— 107 —

Why so much talking about success and not enough walking in it?

— 108 —

Wisdom is simply patience with a lot of practice.

— 109 —

Why is it we teach that if at first you don't succeed, try, try again as if doing it the same way will change things?

— 110 —

Why is it people keep doing stuff the same way, knowing they'll get the same results?

— 111 —

Why is it some people don't have to do anything in particular to be oddballs?

— 112 —

Why is it that gossiping helps some people bond together?

— 113 —

Why is it some people light up the room while others darken it?

POLITICS

Political Misdemeanors

— 1 —

Why is it we use the word 'politics' when it is made up of 'poli' meaning 'many' in Latin, and 'tics' as in 'bloodsucking creatures'?

— 2 —

If crime fighters fight crime and fire fighters fight fire, what do freedom fighters fight?

— 3 —

Why is it making peace is harder than making war?

— 4 —

Some people are free of all prejudices; they hate everyone equally.

— 5 —

They say that only one in four rapes are reported. How do they know?

— 6 —

What do mandatory options and mutual differences mean? It's like all talk and no commitment.

— 7 —

What level of importance must a person have, before they are considered assassinated instead of just murdered?

— 8 —

Who says we can't turn left on red?

— 9 —

Why can't they make black Barbie dolls look like black people and not like white folks?

— 10 —

Why do most cars have speedometers that go up to at least 130 when you legally can't go that fast on any road?

— 11 —

Why does it take a whole county to get one man? Like Saddam Hussein?

— 12 —

Why is it America feels white collar is superior to blue collar crime?

— 13 —

Why is it America aids others before helping our own American citizens?

— 14 —

Why is it America supports and encourages pornography by calling it freedom of speech and expression?

— 15 —

Why is it America supports and even designs sex education programs for all school grade levels, provides students with condoms but refuses to address racism?

— **16** —

Why is it America's so fascinated with the sexual behavior of their politicians?

— **17** —

Why is it Americans accept responsibility for only the good decisions the government makes?

— **18** —

Why is it Americans are such sensationalists?

— **19** —

Why is a person who plays the piano called a pianist, but a person who drives a race car not called a racist?

— **20** —

Why is it no one will admit they're in politics because they like to argue and fight over who's the boss?

— **21** —

Why is it few politicians can give a straight answer or make a straight face but they all want your vote?

— **22** —

Why it is no one wants to listen?

— **23** —

Why is it the United States would rather be divided than united?

POLITICS

Part 2

A Piece of Mind in the Name of Peace

— **1** —

Why is it Americans are treated badly in other countries but America allows foreigners to do almost anything?

— **2** —

Why is it Americans only go to the circus in the hopes of seeing some horrendous accident?

— **3** —

Why is it an English accent is considered romantic, but a southern accent is considered illiterate?

— **4** —

Why is it anti-abortionists feel it's OK to kill?

— **5** —

Why is it everybody wants to lead but nobody wants to follow?

— 6 —

Why is it freedom of speech has become the power to pollute, deface, demoralize, destroy and dehumanize?

— 7 —

Why is it freedom of speech is used more frequently than freedom of thought?

— 8 —

Why is it that freedom is only relative?

— 9 —

Why is friendly fire appreciated by everybody except the dead guy?

— 10 —

Why is it IRS auditors take such pleasure in hurting the little man?

— 11 —

Why is it legal documents which should clear up confusion, make it worse?

— 12 —

Why is it legal for cops to speed limit and run traffic lights at will?

— 13 —

Why is it medals are given in casualties of war but one on one killings are rewarded with jail time.

— 14 —

Why is it meter readers get such a thrill out of writing a parking ticket?

— 15 —

Why is it no matter how good your driving record, the insurance company won't give you a break?

— 16 —

Why is it older people matter when it's time to vote but not when it's time to adjust the economy?

— 17 —

Why is it our laws are designed to persecute the victim and victimize the persecuted?

— 18 —

Why is it our laws are designed to protect the convicted, criminal and the criminally insane instead of the victim?

— 18 —

Why is it people sit on the Hill making decisions about people they know nothing about? Is that the value of government?

— 19 —

Why don't we admit that politics is a game between those who have and those who don't want others to have?

— 20 —

Why is it a secret can only be kept if two of three people who know it are dead?

— 21 —

Why don't we get paid for the things we like to do?

— 22 —

Why is it used car salesman yell on commercials but Mercedes Benz dealers whisper?

— 23 —

Why is it that lazy people always want to be in the spotlight?

— 24 —

If quitters never win, and winners never quit, who came up with, "Quit while you're still ahead?"

POLITICS

Part 3

Room for Everybody at the Booth

— **1** —

Why is it people think it's a great day in America when a great leader gets accused of sexual harassment?

— **2** —

Why is it people think it's OK to keep money they find if it was lost by a large corporation?

— **3** —

Why is it people who follow the rules get recognized less frequently than those who break the rules?

— **4** —

Why is it racism has to carry people to their graves?

— **5** —

Why is it Rastafarian hair styles freak out some people?

— **6** —

Why is it religion and government contribute to violence when that's what they both should be combating?

— **7** —

Why is it so hard to get health insurance when you have a pre-existing condition?

— **8** —

Why is it so hard to update American educational programs and classroom reading materials for cultural diversity?

— **9** —

Why is it that the media is exempt from criticism and above the law?

— **10** —

Why is it the law refuses to intervene and help citizens until a criminal act has been committed?

— 11 —

Why is it the media feels it's their job to let the would-be murderer know that he didn't get his victim?

— 12 —

Why is it the media felt it necessary to film the war and run it live during prime time hours?

— 13 —

Why is it the media is allowed without penalty to destroy innocent people's lives?

— 14 —

Why is it the media makes heroes out of glory seekers?

— 15 —

Why is it the media thinks freedom of the press means freedom of irresponsibility?

— **16** —

Why is it the media thinks the public needs to know everything?

— **17** —

Why is it the political parties think running each other down is good?

— **18** —

Why is it when in Rome we do as the Romans do but in America, anything goes?

— **19** —

Why, in the land of freedom and opportunity, is it Americans are never satisfied?

— **20** —

Why is it we cross our fingers and hope to die?

— 21 —

Why is it the more nipping and tucking, the less satisfaction?

— 22 —

Why it is some people live and enjoy as if there is no tomorrow but others live as if there is no today?

— 23 —

Why is it honor and patronage is leaving men once held in esteem?

— 24 —

Why is it one social group is dumb enough to think oppressing another is a good thing?

— 25 —

Why is it society is ok with leadership telling lies?

"

God gave us the gift of life; it is up to us to give ourselves the gift of living well.

Voltaire

RELATIONSHIPS

Therapy of the Sexes

— 1 —

Do guys really think it's okay to wear the same underwear three days in a row?

— 2 —

A successful man makes more than his wife can spend but the successful woman spends quicker than he can make it.

— 3 —

Why is it good words cost nothing?

— 4 —

How come you never hear father-in-law jokes?

— 5 —

How is it possible that someone that you don't even know exists, is in love with you?

— 6 —

Why do husbands and wives look alike yet only the men look like their dogs?

— 7 —

Why is it easier to get what you don't want than what you plan?

— 8 —

Lead me not into temptation; I can find it myself.

— 9 —

Only men who are not interested in women are interested in women's clothes.

— 10 —

Why is it people never complain about fathers-in-law?

— **11** —

Why is it folk who don't understand sexual harassment manage to be so good at it?

— **12** —

Should women who were head of the house have to pay alimony?

— **13** —

Shouldn't a French kiss be when you peck someone on either cheek?

— **14** —

Some people are meant to stay in your heart but you might need to get them out of your life!

— **15** —

What makes late night phone calls last longer?

— **16** —

Why are his-and-her presents always for her?

— **17** —

Why do house guests blame the wife if the place is in shambles?

— **18** —

Why do little men need big women?

— **19** —

Why do men have difficulty understanding the word "no" but they get words like "hydraulics"?

— **20** —

Why do men keep missing the point?

— **21** —

Why do women feel they have to "raise" men?

— 22 —

Why do women have to dress their men?

— 23 —

Why do women think it's better to go to a female gynecologist?

— 24 —

Why do women tolerate "you guys" when men would never go for "you girls"?

— 25 —

Why does it take boys less time in the bathroom than girls?

— 26 —

Why is it women think the fate of the world rests on their shoulders?

— 27 —

Why is it men think women can't drive without them?

— 28 —

Why is it words that deal with intimate female problems are prefaced or suffixed with the word "men". For example: menopause, menstruation, hymen, etc. Or with "hys" (his)? For example, hysteria, hysterectomy, etc. What's any of it got to do with men?

— 29 —

Why is it a guy will fall for a woman even if he knows she's a phony?

— 30 —

Why is it a man claims he'll do anything - but he won't have a vasectomy?

— 31 —

Why is it a man tells her way too much?

— 32 —

Why is it a mother's work is never done?

— 33 —

Why is it a woman expects a man to read her mind?

— 34 —

Why is it a woman goes through 9 months of pain but he can't make it through a headache?

— 35 —

Why is it a woman's intuition is usually right?

— 36 —

Why is it advertisers always pick smiley faced women to advertise women's personal products?

— 37 —

Why is it after centuries with her, men still do not understand women?

— 38 —

Why is it all of the women's physical examination tools are so degrading, probing and painfully intimate in nature?

— 39 —

Why is it couples trust perfect strangers with their most intimate secrets?

— 40 —

Why is it divorce lasts longer and is more successful than marriage?

— 41 —

Why is it doctors think pregnant women about to deliver can scoot from one delivery table to the next?

— 42 —

Why is it easier for someone standing on the outside to see better on the inside?

— **43** —

Why is it easier for women than men to say something negative?

— **44** —

Why is it easier to be a lover than a spouse?

— **45** —

Why is it easier to fall for someone that we know nothing about than someone we know everything about?

— **46** —

Why is it easier to take out frustrations and anger on those we love?

— **47** —

Why is it everybody thinks the worse when a man and woman check into a hotel together?

— 48 —

Why is it everything seems to boil down to the male's lower body?

— 49 —

Why is it fat men want skinny women?

— 50 —

Why is it friendships can stand the test of time, but not marriages?

— 51 —

Why is it guys come out of the bathroom smiling and the women come out frowning?

— 52 —

Why is it harder to tell what gender a person is these days?

— 53 —

Why is it men who like women never notice what they wear?

— 54 —

Why do men always look the same when they come back from the barber?

— 55 —

Why is it people can't just leave the old junk with their Ex?

— 56 —

Why is it some people are born to die and other die to live?

— 57 —

Why is if people snoop through their mates things?

— 58 —

Why is it people expect growth without discomfort?

RELATIONSHIPS

Part 2

His or Hers: It's All Good!

— 1 —

Why is it he says he loves your gray hair but only ogles women without it?

— 2 —

Why is it making up is much sweeter after an argument?

— 3 —

Why is it married couples have separate bank accounts?

— 4 —

Why is it married couples take counsel from someone who's never been married?

— 5 —

Why is it married men hate their wedding bands?

— 6 —

Why is it married women hate single women?

— 7 —

Why is it men always let the woman handle the birth control?

— 8 —

Why is it men are more interested in sex before marriage but women are more interested after?

— 9 —

Why is it woman's intelligence threatens men's egos?

— 10 —

Why is it men tie down women before marriage then feel tied down after marriage?

— 11 —

Why is it men hate asking directions unless a good looking woman is involved?

— 12 —

Why is it men have problems expressing affection in public?

— 13 —

Why is it men haven't figured out yet that insulting women may work; but not in a positive way?

— 14 —

Why is it men justify their unscrupulous behavior based on genes but women justify their behavior based on jeans?

— 15 —

Why is it men spend as much time at the barber's as women even though they have less hair?

— 16 —

Why is it men think it's OK for them to be sloppy but not their women?

— 17 —

Why is it men think talking dirty impresses women?

— 18 —

Why is it men wear the pants but women bear the weight?

— 19 —

Why is it men won't admit when they're lost?

— 20 —

Why is it no matter how much you both desire it, you can not rush love?

— 21 —

Why is it nobody wants to give their real opinion until after the wedding?

— 22 —

Why is it one day you wake up and don't recognize your spouse?

— **23** —

Why is it one second a man is catcalling and whistling at a woman and the next second he's hurling insults at her?

— **24** —

Why is it only one person remembers the anniversary?

— **25** —

Why is it overweight wives tolerate "fat jokes" from sloppy husbands?

— **26** —

Why is it people always wait for the other person to call?

— **27** —

Why is it people are fascinated with silicone implants?

— **28** —

Why is it people don't understand you can love them better if you can breathe?

— **29** —

Why is it people think exchanging the vows changes the guy's behavior?

— **30** —

Why is it people think getting married will change a person?

— **31** —

Why is it people treat their friends worse than acquaintances?

— **32** —

Why is it people value money more than friendships, health and happiness?

— **33** —

Why is it romance can be so depressing sometimes?

— **34** —

Why is it she's called jealous when she spots him checking out a chick, but in a turnabout, he's "protective"?

— 35 —

Why is it slamming doors in people's faces feel so good sometimes?

— 36 —

Why is it sloppy overweight husbands give "lose weight or else" ultimatums to their overweight wives?

— 37 —

Why is it so difficult for people to change?

— 38 —

Why is it so easier to hurt the one you love?

— 39 —

Why is it so easy for a woman to do ten chores to a man's one?

— 40 —

Why is it so easy to attract someone you don't want?

— 41 —

Why is it so hard to give gifts a person likes but so easy to give what we either love or hate?

— 42 —

Why is it so hard to let go?

— 43 —

Why is it so hard to move on, even after your feelings are gone?

— 44 —

Why is it some women give up on all men just because one guy messed up?

— 45 —

Why is it some people don't know who their real friends are?

— 46 —

Why is it some people fight over the check?

— 47 —

Why is it some people ruin a good divorce by getting remarried?

— 48 —

Why is it some women call their men dogs?

— 49 —

Why is it some women feel the way to park the car in a tiny space is to tap the car in front and back?

— 50 —

Why is it some women get happy when their girlfriend's marriage is on the rocks?

— 51 —

Why is it that a woman will give up all of her friends for a guy she just met at the bus stop?

— 52 —

Why is it that as soon as you get engaged, interesting people start coming out of the woodwork and everybody you meet looks good to you?

— 53 —

Why is it that as soon as you're ready to settle down, your significant other is not?

— 54 —

Why is it she's always gotta put in her two cents worth?

— 55 —

Why is it we keep expecting one of the fruit loops to taste different?

RELATIONSHIPS

Part 3

Too Many Walls; Not Enough Bridges

— 1 —

Why is it that he complains, but she nags?

— 2 —

Why is it that instead of giving up when the catcall didn't work, man invented other things equally as obnoxious like honking horns and shouting verbal insults?

— 3 —

Why is it that it takes 6 months to plan the wedding and it's all over in an hour?

— 4 —

Why is it that it takes 6 months to plan the wedding but the ceremony lasts 1 hour, the honeymoon lasts 1 month and the marriage lasts 1 year?

— 5 —

Why is it that when a woman accidentally runs over the curb, she's a screw-up but when he does it, he was testing tire pressure or wheel alignment?

— 6 —

Why is it that when she speeds she's being reckless but when he does it, he's in a hurry?

— 7 —

Why is it that women, the weaker sex, can be more deadly than men?

— 8 —

Why is it the bride is always late for something she's been planning for months?

— 9 —

Why is it the men's bathroom is always so much neater than the ladies'?

— 10 —

Why is it the mother has to go through so much more than the father?

— 11 —

Why is it the mother who keeps the family together?

— 12 —

Why is it the one person that catches your eye is already spoken for?

— 13 —

Why is it the person being "fought over" doesn't care about either party involved in the fight?

— 14 —

Why is it the relationship is OK until a woman tells somebody else about him?

— 15 —

Why is it the relationship was fine until he borrowed money from you?

— 16 —

Why is it the women get it but the men don't?

— 17 —

Why is it the women who can't keep their dresses down always complain when the guys look?

— 18 —

Why is it there is always a line in the Ladies bathroom?

— 19 —

Why is it they always announce marriages but not divorces?

— 20 —

Why is it we do what naturally tempts a man and then expect him not be tempted?

— 21 —

Why is it we make many long last friendships very easily when we're kids, but when we grow up we can hardly make new acquaintances?

— 22 —

Why is it when a woman loses weight, her friends suddenly point out how unhealthy weight loss can be?

— 23 —

Why is it when a woman makes the first move, she's considered desperate?

— 24 —

Why is it when a woman pays a man to examine her, he's called a gynecologist but when a man pays a woman for the same thing, she's called a hooker?

— 25 —

Why is it when one of you is in love, the other is not?

— 26 —

Why is it when you finally get flowers, they're from the wrong person?

— 27 —

Why is it when you finally get your heart's desire, you're miserable?

— 28 —

Why is it wives don't every buy men vacuum cleaners?

— 29 —

Why is it women are always examining the relationship?

— 30 —

Why is it women are good friends until a man enters the room?

— 31 —

Why is it women blame car breakdowns on their husbands?

— 32 —

Why is it women can shop until they drop but men are done at the first stop?

— 33 —

Why is it women cry about everything?

— 34 —

Why is it women don't get motivated to clean house until a man's coming to visit?

— 35 —

Why is it women feel like they have to be superwoman to get respect?

— 36 —

Why is it women find it hard to compliment other women on a new outfit?

— 37 —

Why is it women find it hard to pay other women genuine compliments?

— 38 —

Why is it women forget how to drive and take out trash after they get married?

— 39 —

Why is it women get hair styles that require them to sleep with their heads hanging off the bed?

— **40** —

Why is it women get mad with their men for dreaming?

— **41** —

Why is it women go to the bathroom in pairs at work?

— **42** —

Why is it women have to raise their voices to get their point across?

— **43** —

Why is it women readily crucify men for certain indiscretions but make allowances for themselves when they commit the same transgressions?

— **44** —

Why is it women spend ridiculous money on high maintenance hairdos?

— 45 —

Why is it women spend so much money on panty hose when they tear with one wear?

— 46 —

Why is it women take so long in the bathroom?

— 47 —

Why is it women think feeling bad gives them license to take it out on anybody in their path?

— 48 —

Why is it women think of themselves as very subtle but men as crudely obvious?

— 49 —

Why is it women wait until they are in the high speed lane to put on their mascara?

— 50 —

Why is it women wear clothes to get attention but when they get the wrong kind of attention, they deny the clothes were a factor?

— 51 —

Why is it women's bathroom lines are always longer than the men's?

— 52 —

Why is it you can never pinpoint when you became friends with somebody; you just know it happened?

— 53 —

Why is it you can never remember the birthday of the one friend you have who always remembers yours?

— 54 —

Why is it you can't get to know a person until you marry them?

— 55 —

Why is it you really don't know your mate until you're married and have a quarrel?

— 56 —

Why is it people start a relationship with someone still living with an ex?

— 57 —

Why do friends think it's ok to eavesdrop on your conversation and then discuss what they overheard with you?

— 58 —

Why is it fighting over the same things: money, sex, work, parenting and housework can split up some but build up others?

RELIGION

Let the Church Say Amen!

— 1 —

A bad attitude is like a flat tire; you're not going anywhere until you change it.

— 2 —

Why is it black people will sit under a white man's ministry but white people won't sit under a black man's ministry?

— 3 —

Adam blamed Eve, Eve blamed the serpent and the serpent didn't have a leg to stand on.

— 4 —

Why is it Christians are so judgmental?

— 5 —

Do you feel you have a purpose or calling in life?

— **6** —

Who do fools rush in where angels fear to tread?

— **7** —

Give a man a fish, and you'll feed him for a day; give him a religion, and he'll starve to death while praying for a fish.

— **8** —

God loves to rescue us when we're on our last legs.

— **9** —

God wants spiritual fruit, not religious nuts.

— **10** —

Going to church doesn't make you a Christian any more than going to the garage makes you a car.

— 11 —

Good people spend so much time fighting the devil they forget what love is and how to make peace.

— 12 —

How come it's easier to hear God when you can't go anywhere or do anything?

— 13 —

How is it that the same truth that will set you free, will almost kill you first?

— 14 —

If an atheist has to go to court, do they make him swear on the Bible?

— 15 —

If charity starts at home, why do people have to leave town to find somebody in need?

— 16 —

If God doesn't like the way I live, let him tell me, not you.

— 17 —

If God intended to make us all the same, why is one person's craziness another person's reality?

— 18 —

If the battle is in the mind, why is the war so important?

— 19 —

If the mind can achieve what it can conceive and believe, what else matters?

— 20 —

If the whole universe has no meaning, we should never have found out that it has no meaning.

— 21 —

Why is it ministers require more of you than God?

— 22 —

Why is it ministers think they have more authority than God?

— 23 —

Morality is doing what is right, no matter what you are told; while religion is doing what you are told, no matter what is right.

— 24 —

If no one should judge us, how can anyone else judge God's creation and call it bad?

— 25 —

One sure fire way to fail is to please everybody all the time.

— 26 —

Why is it people acknowledge God when He says "yes" but deny Him otherwise?

— 27 —

People have just enough religion to make us hate, but not enough to make us love one another.

— 28 —

Why is it people measure everything by their personal standards?

— 29 —

People say they commit their crime and child abuse in the name of God or Jesus, but never Satan.

— 30 —

Why do saved folk claim God doesn't come when you want Him but yet He's right on time?

— 31 —

Why is it saved folk always rush God?

— 32 —

Why do some people lose common sense the minute they get saved?

— 33 —

Some think gift giving has to be of a physical nature.

— 34 —

Why is the congregation full of women but mostly men in the pulpit and on the board?

— 35 —

Why is the focus more on membership than soul winning?

— 36 —

Why do preachers yell “at” absent members to those who’re present?

— **37** —

Why do the pastor's wife runs the church?

— **38** —

God uses people who irritate you and suddenly, you grow up!

— **39** —

Why is it pastors mostly like go to church to preach but don't like to come to receive input?

— **40** —

Why is it folk talk about what Jesus would do and then promptly do something else?

— **41** —

Why is it Christianity's starting to feel more like a bait and switch rather than hope eternal?

— 42 —

Why is it pastors who do not have enough time for their members keep looking for more members?

— 43 —

Why do churches totally run by older people expect younger people to participate?

— 44 —

Why is it folk act as though Christians should always be cheerful?

— 45 —

Why is it weird stuff seems to happen only to certain people in the church?

— 46 —

Why is it men don't admit that they'd rather the Lord didn't make them a better man because they're having too much fun as they are?

— **47** —

Why is it the kids would rather stay with you than to be brought up in a Christian home?

— **48** —

Why is it your sense of humor is the first thing to go after conversion?

— **49** —

Why is it people's ego always gets in the way?

— **50** —

Why it is some people prefer war over peace?

— **51** —

Why is it people are suspicious of free stuff?

RELIGION

Part 2

God Has Spoken!

— 1 —

Why is it we ask God for something and then tell him how to give it to us?

— 2 —

Why is it we ask questions that don't have an answer?

— 3 —

Who killed the dead sea?

— 4 —

Why are there so many "Do Not" than "Do" rules in church?

— 5 —

Why can't folk stay awake when the preacher's up?

— 6 —

Why do so many of us think God needs us?

— 7 —

Why do they say death brings us closer to life?

— 8 —

Why does God have to repeat so much stuff in the Bible?

— 9 —

Why does religion cause so much war?

— 10 —

Why is it atheists constantly seek to disprove God's existence?

— 11 —

Why is it Christians forget the Word when they need it most?

— 12 —

Why is it churches are so competitive?

— **13** —

Why is it churches tend to forget that every man must get to heaven based on individual merit?

— **14** —

Why is it easier to be merciless when you get mercy?

— **15** —

Why is it easier to confer with a stranger on the street than to counsel with the minister?

— **16** —

Why is it easier to fight than be at peace?

— **17** —

Why is it easier to preach than practice?

— **18** —

Why is it easier to talk to God than your pastor?

— 19 —

Why is it everybody talks about finding Jesus as if he was lost or something?

— 20 —

Why is it everybody thinks missionary work is something you do only in some foreign land?

— 21 —

Why is it everybody wants to go to heaven but nobody wants to die?

— 22 —

Why is it families who stay together have to do more than pray?

— 23 —

Why is it man scorns the meek and lowly?

— 24 —

Why is it more popular to be involved in secular activities than religious ones?

— **25** —

Why is it Mother Theresa who gave her life for humanity, was judged unclean and not fit to sit at the table with the elite?

— **26** —

Why is it no matter how little the value of the dollar bill is, the rich still have more money but the poor have more love?

— **27** —

Why is it pastors talk a lot about love until the candidate joins church, then he talks otherwise.

— **28** —

Why is it people are shocked when they get what they prayed for?

— **29** —

Why is it people are so busy trying to get to Church they don't have time to enjoy church?

— **30** —

Why is it people call you stupid for being honest?

— **31** —

Why is it people can get their feelings so easily hurt at church but take all sorts of lip from people on the job and say nothing?

— **32** —

Why is it people feel like they're doing the minister a favor by showing up at church?

— **33** —

Why is it people have to be almost dead to get a good Samaritan to stop by?

— **34** —

Why is it people hold grudges so long they can't remember the reason?

— **35** —

Why is it people hold their leaders to a higher standard than themselves?

— **36** —

Why is it people insist upon wrestling with their conscience?

— **37** —

Why is it people keep winning members to church but not to Christ?

— **38** —

Why is it people think a man of the cloth is a man of steel?

— **39** —

Why is it people who are stingy with their offerings are so demanding?

— 40 —

Why is it preachers yell or holler during their sermons?

— 41 —

If Solomon was so wise, why is it preachers don't preach out of the Book of Solomon?

— 42 —

Why is it religion makes people forget that they are just people, too?

— 43 —

Why is it people don't realize that Jesus wasn't religious?

— 44 —

Why is it that as much time has passed, that religion isn't what makes people live right?

RELIGION

Part 3

Hit or Miss

I need someone to sign for these.

— 1 —

Why is it people who claim they don't believe in God always ask him for help when they're in trouble?

— 2 —

Why is it people who lay down their lives for others are treated with little fanfare during their lifetime?

— 3 —

Why is it people who talk about the joy of the Lord seem so miserable?

— 4 —

Why is it preachers have the rules together except where their kids are concerned?

— 5 —

Why is it Princess Diana received so more tributes following her death than Mother Theresa?

— **6** —

Why is it so hard to stay awake in church?

— **7** —

Why is it so easy for the pastor to remember and speak on all the bad things that his members do?

— **8** —

Why is it so easy to yield to temptation?

— **9** —

Why is it so hard for Choir Directors to dismiss a person who can't sing?

— **10** —

Why is it so hard to get men to go to church?

— **11** —

Why is it many pastors act as if they think God's shoes are replaceable?

— 12 —

Why is it so many religious folk are poor?

— 13 —

Why is it some people are so religious they don't have time for God?

— 14 —

Why is it some people go through hell before they die and some people go through it after?

— 15 —

Why is it some people never hear when God says "NO"?

— 16 —

Why is it television networks are quick to post disclaimers on religious programs but not for sexually suggestive or provocative ads?

— **17** —

Why is it the same guy that said he's going to have an air sandwich and a glass of wind, has six in one hand and half a dozen in the other?

— **18** —

Why is it that people who want to share their religious views with you, almost never want you to share yours with them?

— **19** —

Why is it the God gives us a choice but the church doesn't?

— **20** —

Why is it gray haired grandmothers makes us feel secure?

— **21** —

Why is it the minister always asks you if you remembered last Sunday's sermon?

— 22 —

Why is it the offering plate has to be passed four or five times at church?

— 23 —

Why is it the Pastor's opinion seems more important than God's word?

— 24 —

Why is it the Pastors will only attend if he's the Pastor?

— 25 —

Why is it the people who can't carry a tune are the ones who're first in line to join the choir?

— 26 —

Why is it the very people who keep breaking their promises to God get upset if He doesn't hear them?

— **27** —

Why is it there isn't a lot of laughter in the Bible?

— **28** —

Why is it there's a church on almost every street corner but the city is still full of sinners?

— **29** —

Why is it we can get up and go wherever we want anytime of day or night in any kind of weather until it's time to go to church?

— **30** —

Why is it we cannot appreciate the equality of all humanity? We're nothing but dirt.

— **31** —

Why is it we take ourselves so seriously if we are just dust of the earth?

— 32 —

Why is it we think everything has to be fair?

— 33 —

Why is it we try to get God to accept our religion?

— 34 —

Why is it we're always telling people to go where we don't want to go?

— 35 —

Why is it we're never satisfied with what we have?

— 36 —

Why is it when part of the body hurts, the rest of the body feels it?

— 37 —

Why is that people seldom believe that the Bible means what it says: instead they think it means what they say?

— 38 —

Why it is so easy to judge others but not ourselves?

— 39 —

Why will devoted followers support a leader at the expense of their family?

— 40 —

Why is it some people don't believe in God but do believe in voodoo?

— 41 —

Why is it many people say they have faith but do not know what they really believe or why?

Success is Ok; Happiness is Better

— 1 —

If a book about failures doesn't sell, is it a success?

— 2 —

If money doesn't grow on trees then why do banks have branches?

— 3 —

Isn't it funny in an oxymoronic way how skinny people are so stingy?

— 4 —

Why is a person who handles money called a broker?

— 5 —

Why is it people pay for what they want and beg for what they need?

— 6 —

Why is it a carpenter's house is never finished?

— 7 —

Why is it doctors can't write?

— 8 —

Why is it folk at the office think you can keep up with everybody's email conversation?

— 9 —

Why is it we suffer sociologically for every technological success?

— 10 —

Why is it large sums of lost money has a way of finding it's way into the wrong hands?

— 11 —

Why is it lawyering has become more about lying than lawyering?

— 12 —

Why is it many producers feel it's ok to show the female anatomy totally nude but not the male?

— 13 —

Why is it money always brings people back home?

— 14 —

Why is it no matter how much money some people have, they're always broke?

— 15 —

Why is it no matter how much money you make, it's never enough?

— 16 —

Why is it nobody thinks of taking out their happiness on somebody?

— 17 —

Why is it nobody cares about anything anymore?

— 18 —

Why is it more people define the outcome they want first, and then reverse engineer what's needed to get there?

— 19 —

If the top speed of the first American car race in 1895 was 7 mph, why is it we are not satisfied driving over 100 mph?

— 20 —

Why is it we don't laugh more knowing that laughing boosts the immune system, burns calories and reduces stress hormones?

— 21 —

Why is it some people would rather work longer hours at a slower pace than shorter hours at a faster pace?

SUCCESS

Part 2

Reaching for Low Hanging Fruit

— 1 —

Why is it optimism lasts only a few days at a time but pessimism lasts forever?

— 2 —

Why is it people who hate house cleaning have the biggest houses?

— 3 —

Why is it people will give their last dime to a slot machine?

— 4 —

Why is it rebates never come in the mail as promised?

5 —

Why is it so difficult to set the microwave clocks in this new age of technology?

— 6 —

Why is it so hard to get a real person on the phone about your money?

— 7 —

Why is it some people spend more money on their cars than they do on their houses?

— 8 —

Why is it some people would put owning a car over owning a home?

— 9 —

Why is it that people dwell on sorrow forever but forget their victories in a day?

— 10 —

Why is it the less we know, the longer it takes to explain it?

— 11 —

Why is it the naturally "good things" in life are going bad?

— 12 —

Why is it that the same people get scammed over and over?

— 13 —

Why is it the smaller the sports car, the more expensive the price tag?

— 14 —

Why is it the waiter's job to figure out who gets the check?

— 15 —

Why is it they always tell you "they just sold the last one" when you race out to catch the sale?

— 16 —

Why is it they can always find you to get money but they can never find you to pay you back?

— 17 —

Why is it so easy to forget how we climbed the ladder of success?

— 18 —

Why is it people forget where diamonds come from when they see one they like?

— 19 —

Why is it the winning the game is not the success but how the game was played?

— 20 —

Why is it many lottery winners still lose?

— 21 —

Why is it folk don't understand what true riches is?

SUCCESS

Part 3

Not All It's Cracked Up to Be

— **1** —

Why is it we get lazier, tardier and slower when the latest technology is meant to make us more efficient and productive?

— **2** —

Why is it we value things less if stuff comes easy?

— **3** —

Why is it what's good for you tastes bad and what's bad for you tastes good?

— **4** —

Why is it when you don't take a 2 for 1 deal, you get penalized and they charge you twice as much for buying just one?

— **5** —

Why is it wise people say little but fools always have so much to say?

— 6 —

Why is the meaning of life hard to find when you have a dictionary?

— 7 —

Why is there so much red tape to everything?

— 8 —

Why is your definition of true happiness different from anyone else's definition of true happiness?

— 9 —

Why worry about what people think about you? It's none of your business...

— 10 —

Winners are not afraid of losing but losers are afraid of winning.

— 11 —

Isn't it ironic that you cannot get anything clean without first getting something else dirty?

— 12 —

Why is it you can't miss what you don't have?

— 13 —

Why do you get tired when you exercise but not when you play sports?

— 14 —

You should respect when people are jealous of you, they think you are better than them.

— 15 —

How is it that problems go away faster when you stop thinking about them?

— **16** —

A thief is successful only in familiar places.

— **17** —

Why is it success comes overnight to some folk who put in little effort but never comes to those who worked hard?

— **18** —

Why is it some people make it to the top only to topple over?

— **19** —

Why is it two people can have strength and knowledge, but one fails simply because of lack of will?

— **20** —

Why is it we forget to be thankful that we did not get what we wanted?

TRANSITIONING

Out of the Box Thinking

— 1 —

Why is it nobody thinks of taking out their happiness on somebody?

— 2 —

Do they put underwear on corpses?

— 3 —

Do you believe that dreams can be messages from a "higher level"?

— 4 —

Everything will be alright in the end; so if it is not alright, it is not the end.

— 5 —

If a chronic liar tells you he is a chronic liar do you believe him?

— 6 —

If a deaf person has to go to court, is it still called a hearing?

— **7** —

If a synchronized swimmer drowns, does her partner also have to drown?

— **8** —

If an ambulance is on its way to save someone, and it runs someone over, does it stop to help them?

— **9** —

If ghosts go through walls, why don't they fall through the floor?

— **10** —

If heat rises, then shouldn't hell be cold?

— **11** —

If I save time, when do I get it back?

— **12** —

If life is pleasant and death is so peaceful, why is the transition so troublesome?

— 13 —

If old people poke you at weddings and say "You're next"; should you poke them at funerals?

— 14 —

If the folks at the psychic hotlines were really psychic, wouldn't they call you first?

— 15 —

Why are there flotation device under plane seats, instead of parachutes?

— 16 —

If you woke up one day and found that you have become invisible, what is the first thing that you would do?

— 17 —

Why do coffins have lifetime guarantees?

— 18 —

Why do they call it quicksand when it sucks you down slowly?

— 19 —

Why does the weekend always go by too fast?

— 20 —

Why don't the family of a murder victim get to have any say in what punishment is given?

— 21 —

Why is it funny to hear someone say somebody "got hit by a bus"?

— 22 —

Why is it people go to jail for committing a mercy killing?

— 23 —

Why is it the dark cloud only hangs over your head?

— 24 —

Why is it called alcoholics anonymous when the first thing you do is stand, blab your name and tell all your business?

— 25 —

Why is it advice sounds good until somebody you hate says it?

— 26 —

Why is it after you grow up and move away, everything looks so small when you go back?

— 27 —

Why is it a cop gone bad gets treated better than a private citizen?

— 28 —

Why is it considered lying when you're acting for real?

— 29 —

Why is it considered necessary to nail down the lid of a coffin?

— 30 —

Why is it everybody has a nosey neighbor?

— 31 —

Why is it the words are on the tip of your tongue but you still can't catch them?

— 32 —

If mid-wives deliver babies, what do mid-men, the male versions do?

— 33 —

Why is it church feels more like a social club than a faith community?

— **35** —

Why is it people still fool with mistletoe despite the myth that you will not marry if you don't honor it?

— **36** —

Why is it man does not eat more insects if they are so nutritious?

— **37** —

Why is it weird stuff seems to happen only to certain people?

— **38** —

Why is it that just before you doze off into a peaceful sleep you feel like you're falling off a cliff?

— **39** —

Why is it recurring dreams never seem to be about stuff we want to enjoy over and over?

TRANSITIONING

Part 2

Move Over or Move On

— 1 —

Why is it new cars always wear out just before the last car note?

— 2 —

Why is it no matter how much you try to break certain habits, you just can't?

— 3 —

Why is it death benefits seem so hard to appreciate?

— 4 —

Why do doctors make the worst patients?

— 5 —

Why is it driver's permit photos look like mug shots?

— 6 —

If it takes a lot more muscles to frown, then why does frowning come easier than smiles ?

— 7 —

Why is it elderly licensed drivers press the brake every 20-30 seconds?

— 8 —

Why is it everybody acts like they love you at funerals?

— 9 —

Why is it everybody wants to come to America but when they get here, they try to destroy it?

— 10 —

Why is it everybody wants to surprise you every year on your birthday with a surprise birthday party at your house?

— 11 —

Why is it everything's more confusing, less organized and more time consuming now that we are in the electronic age?

— 12 —

Why is it female gynecologists are rough during exams?

— 13 —

Why is it foreign businesses put people on the customer service desk who cannot speak English?

— 14 —

Why is it funerals bring out the best in people?

— 15 —

Why is it funerals never start on time even though the special guest is already present?

— 16 —

Why is it house cleaning depends on whether or not someone's coming?

— **17** —

Why is it illegal to park in a handicapped zone but ok to use handicapped toilet?

— **18** —

Why is it in the electronic age, we now have to maintain a hard copy audit trail of what we did electronically?

— **19** —

Why is it life's over before we know it?

— **20** —

Why is it criminals are permitted to profit off their crimes in some states?

— **21** —

Why is it criminals who trust other criminals are shocked when their partners in crime betray them?

— 22 —

Why is it no one respects administrators until a paycheck doesn't show up?

— 23 —

Why is it our life only flashes before our eyes in near death cases?

— 24 —

Why is it people are afraid of the dark and things they cannot see?

— 25 —

Why is it people are always imposing the very punishment they dread on someone else?

— 26 —

Why is it people dread birthdays after 30? The only way to stop them is to die.

— 27 —

What's wrong with the change of life?

— 28 —

Why is it people say "see you later" when they know they won't?

— 29 —

Why is it folk think you're strange for walking around smiling for no obvious reason?

— 30 —

Why is it so easy to forget how we made it over?

— 31 —

Why is it people forget where diamonds come from when they see one they like?

— 32 —

Why is it the louder some people are in the office they more respect they get?

TRANSITIONING

Part 3

Hanging On by a Thread

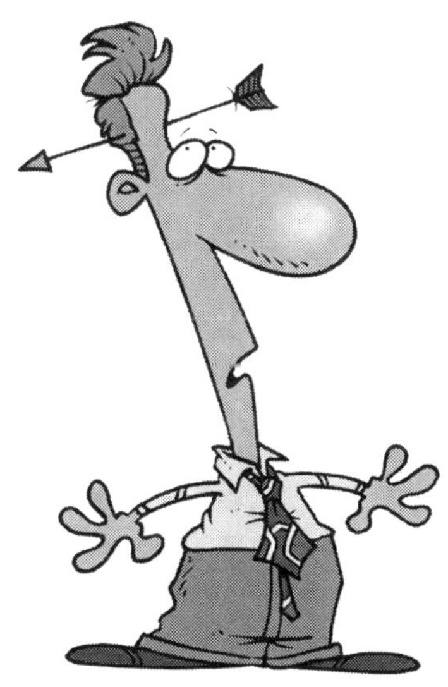

— 1 —

Why is it people who laugh and make sport of others hurt so badly when turnabout's fair play?

— 2 —

Why is it road crews always detour you through some sort of death trap?

— 3 —

Why is it senior citizens insist on driving in the fast lane?

— 4 —

Why is it shocking that Black men have a higher fatality rate when everybody's trying to kill them?

— 5 —

Why is it so easy for hospitals to get away with hurting patients?

— 6 —

Why is it people risk their own safety to watch horror?

— 7 —

Why is it some people go the bathroom, touch their private parts and still won't wash their hands?

— 8 —

Why is it some people know everything except how little their opinions matter?

— 9 —

Why is it that it always takes forever to get home when you're in a hurry?

— 10 —

Why is it the funeral is harder to get through than the initial shock of death?

— 11 —

Why is it the louder one person shouts, the softer the calm person's voice becomes?

— 12 —

Why is it the older a man's age, the higher his pants?

— 13 —

Why is it the perpetrators always return to the scene of the crime?

— 14 —

Why is it they call it a Wake?

— 15 —

Why is it they don't have a senior citizen express lane just for retired people?

— 16 —

Why is it they make the weatherman stand out in the rain, sleet and snow?

— 17 —

Why is it they make you whisper in the morgue?

— 18 —

Why is it we always fall into a deep sleep just before it's time to get up and go to work?

— 19 —

Why is it we only adjust the time and not the whole workday in the winter?

— 20 —

Why is it we're so anxious to let a computer take over our lives?

— 21 —

Why is it when you leave the room to do something, you forget what you were going to do?

— 22 —

Why is the ambulance ride so bumpy?

— 23 —

Why is the time of day with the slowest traffic called rush hour?

— 24 —

Why it is your friends walk off and leave you standing in the middle of the mall talking to yourself? Or worse, a perfect stranger.

— 25 —

Why should coffins need a lifetime guarantee?

— 26 —

Wise people are not always silent, but they do know when to be (silent).

— 27 —

How come one can be overwhelmed and underwhelmed, but why can't you be simply whelmed?

— 28 —

If we have that indestructible black box that is used on planes in one apart of the plan, why can't they make that work for the whole plane?

— 29 —

Why is it we see the same people differently when we get older?

— 30 —

Why is it life never turns out quite like expected?

— 31 —

Why is it man is always tempted to do what he is advised against?

— 32 —

Why is it saints, who deserve recognition, do not want to be pulled into the limelight?

OTHER

Stuff and Nonsense

— 1 —

Are people who are allergic to nuts allergic to coconuts too?

— 2 —

Are there crash courses on how to fly?

— 3 —

Are there pink lemons that make pink lemonade?

— 4 —

Blowing out someone else's candles doesn't make your light shine any brighter.

— 5 —

Borrowing money from a pessimist is better because he won't expect it back.

— 6 —

Can we spell creativity however we want?

— 7 —

Can you "zone out" and be "in the zone" at the same time?

— 8 —

Can you be put you under house arrest if you live in a mobile home?

— 9 —

Can you cry under water?

— 10 —

Can you get cornered in a round room?

— 11 —

Does wild rice have to be hunted?

— 12 —

Funny how we can squeeze bread but we cannot unsqueeze it.

— 13 —

How can a cable be wireless?

— 14 —

How can bright people can be so stupid but stupid people can't ever be bright?

— 15 —

How can something be both "new" and "improved" – if it's new, what was being improved?

— 16 —

How come only your fingers and toes get all wrinkled in the bathtub?

— 17 —

How come Superman's chest stops bullets, but he ducks when someone throws a gun?

— 18 —

How come when you call a wrong number, someone always picks up?

— **19** —

How come you play at a recital, but recite at a play?

— **20** —

How come you press harder on a remote control when you know the battery is dead?

— **21** —

How do ideas come out of nowhere?

— **22** —

How do they determine calories for a stick of gum since we only chew and don't swallow it?

— **23** —

How do you know when you have run out of invisible ink?

— **24** —

How far east can you go before you're heading west?

— **25** —

How many times do you use a disposable razor?

— **26** —

If a word is misspelled in the dictionary, how would we ever know?

— **27** —

If an orange is orange, why isn't a lime called a green or a lemon called a yellow?

— **28** —

If it's a truck stop, why do they keep on going?

— **29** —

If it's needless to say, why do people say it?

— **30** —

If quizzes are quizzical then what are tests?

— 31 —

If it's zero degrees outside today and it's supposed to be twice as cold tomorrow, how cold is it going to be?

— 32 —

If nothing ever sticks to Teflon, how do they make Teflon stick to the frying pan?

— 33 —

Why is it we take on the cares of this world instead of giving the world our cares?

— 34 —

If sour cream is past its expiration date is it still good?

— 35 —

If Super Glue is so good why doesn't it stick to the inside of the tube?

— 36 —

If the #2 pencil is the most popular, why's it still #2?

— 37 —

If the plural of tooth is teeth, why isn't the plural of booth beeth?

— 38 —

If the product says "Do not use if seal is broken", how can you open it?

— 39 —

If professor on Gilligan's Island can make a radio out of a coconut, why can't he fix the boat?

— 40 —

If the utensils are gold-plated, should we still consider them silverware?

— 41 —

If you arrest a mime does he have the right to remain silent?

— **42** —

If you can see your breath outside on a cold day, what about expelled gas?

— **43** —

Is it okay to use the AM radio after noon?

— **44** —

Is it really low-fat, or does the serving just fit in the palm of your hand?

— **45** —

Is talk still cheap if you use a lot of ten-dollar words?

— **46** —

Is there another word for synonym?

— **47** —

Isn't the question mark wonderful? Without it, we would take the world for granted.

— 48 —

Laughter may be the best medicine; but laughing for no reason might mean you need the medicine.

— 49 —

Why are loud people so loud?

— 50 —

Why is it fools think they know it all?

— 51 —

Why is it only pharmacists can understand the doctor's writing?

— 52 —

Why is it people don't plan to fail but they fail to plan?

— 53 —

Why is it people only "got a minute" when it's your turn to talk?

— 54 —

Why is it people who've got nothing to say talk non-stop?

— **55** —

Why is it people who make your skin crawl love being around you?

— **56** —

Why is it people who refuse to take baths like hanging with you?

— **57** —

Why is it people who talk a lot hate to listen?

— **58** —

Shouldn't the opposite of shut up be shut down?

— **59** —

Since bread is square, then why is sandwich meat round?

— **60** —

Why is it some people can only listen with their mouths open?

— **61** —

The average man does not know what to do with his life, yet he wants another.

— **62** —

The good thing about being mediocre is always being at your best.

— **63** —

The only way you can fly is to give up things that weigh you down.

— **64** —

The wind blows the ashes back into the face of the one who threw them.

— **65** —

We always get tested on the hard stuff but why is it we never get tested on the easy stuff?

— 66 —

What does "new and improved" say about the old product?

— 67 —

What happens if you put 'this side up' face down while popping microwave popcorn?

— 68 —

What is the opposite of medium?

— 69 —

What makes everybody's ethical when it's convenient?

— 70 —

When people go mental, why do they get physically violent?

— 71 —

When people say, "I'm so tired it's not even funny" or "my head hurts so much it's not even funny", why would it even be funny in the first place?

— 72 —

When someone is yelling at you in sign language, do you just close your eyes so you can "get" it?

— 73 —

Why is it when we get what we want, we don't want it anymore?

— 74 —

When you feel down, why do people ask what's up?

— 75 —

Where does the "o" come from when we abbreviate "number"?

— 76 —

Which is your pleasure - a rose bush with thorns, or thorns with roses?

— **77** —

Who do hospitals security guards get hired to do nothing?

— **78** —

Who says if you make your bed, you have to lie in it? Why can't you remake it or find another bed?

— **79** —

Whose bright idea was it to build homes on a one-way dead-end street?

— **80** —

Why are courtesy cups of water are so tiny?

— **81** —

Why are softballs hard?

— **82** —

Why are the little styrofoam pieces called peanuts?

— 83 —

Why are there signs that read “no shoplifting”? Is there a place where it’s okay?

— 84 —

Why did they put holes in crackers?

— 85 —

Why do ‘a fat chance’ and ‘a slim chance’ mean the same thing?

— 86 —

Why do advertisers specify “free gift”? Aren’t gifts free?

— 87 —

Why do bullies always ask “what’s your problem?” Clearly, they don’t care!

— 88 —

Why do all the light bulbs you installed together go out at different times?

— **89** —

Why do companies offer you "free gifts?" Aren't gifts by definition free?

— **90** —

Why is it nobody wants to go to church anymore?

— **91** —

Why is it easier to say good-bye in the morning?

— **92** —

Why is it society and church folk are so screwed up these days?

— **93** —

Why is it the season is called "fall"?

— **94** —

Why is it many brides are no longer dressing the groom but for the room?

— **95** —

Why is it no one thinks it's strange to remove wisdom teeth?

OTHER

Part 2

Simple Stuff

— 1 —

Why do consumers allow large companies to prey on them?

— 2 —

Why do people pay to go up tall buildings and then put money in binoculars to look down?

— 3 —

Why do folk point to their wrist when asking the time, but don't point to their crotch when asking about the bathroom?

— 4 —

Why do people say "The alarm just went off" when really it just came on?

— 5 —

Why do people say, "You can't have your cake and eat it too"? Why would someone get cake if they can't eat it?

— 6 —

Why do some people never get the point?

— 7 —

Why do some people tell everything?

— 8 —

Why do some people get it but others don't?

— 9 —

Why do the lights go out at the worst times like when you're on the john?

— 10 —

Why do the numbers on phones go down but numbers on calculators go up?

— 11 —

Why do they report power outages on TV?

— 12 —

Why do they make scented toilet paper?

— 13 —

Why do toasters have a setting that burns toast to a horrible crisp that no one eats?

— 14 —

Why do unhappy people go out and hang around a bunch of drunk people on New Year's?

— 15 —

Why do we call something sent by car a shipment and something sent by ship a cargo?

— 16 —

Why do we call them novels when they're mostly unoriginal?

— 17 —

Why do we drive on parkways and park on driveways?

— **18** —

Why do we like imitating other people's accents?

— **19** —

Why do we put shirts in a suitcase, and put suits in a garment bag?

— **20** —

Why do we say "a pair of pants" when there is only one article of clothing involved?

— **21** —

Why do we scrub Down and wash Up?

— **22** —

Why do we sing "Take Me Out to the Ballgame" when we're already there?

— **23** —

Why do we tend to hunch our shoulders when we're out in the rain?

— 24 —

Why do you go "back and forth" to town if you really must go forth before you go back?

— 25 —

Why do you have to wait in five different little rooms before you get to see the doctor?

— 26 —

Why do you press harder on the buttons of a remote control when you know the batteries are dead?

— 27 —

Why do your fingernails break off down to your finger? Ouch!!

— 28 —

Why does 'dyslexia' have to be so hard to spell?

— 29 —

Why does "fat chance" and "slim chance" mean the same thing?

— 30 —

Why does "slow down" and "slow up" mean the same thing?

— 31 —

Why does a round pizza come in a square box?

— 32 —

Why does everybody thinks they have a secret?

— 33 —

Why does grass only smell when you cut it?

— 34 —

Why does it always rain right after you get your hair done?

— 35 —

Why does it take 15 minutes to cook minute rice?

— 36 —

Why does it take a major crisis to get people to listen to you sometimes?

— 37 —

Why does it takes 2 days to end the week?

— 38 —

Why does Jello have a smell when you add the powder in the water, but when it "gels" the scent virtually disappears?

— 39 —

Why does mineral water that has trickled through mountains for centuries have a use by date?

— **40** —

Why does the last piece of ice always stick to the bottom of the cup?

— **41** —

Why does the sun lighten our hair, but darken our skin?

— **42** —

Why does your nose run and your feet smell?

— **43** —

Why doesn't baking soda freeze?

— **44** —

Why don't the hairs on your arms get split ends?

— **45** —

Why don't hair stylist fix their hair?

— **46** —

Why don't nail biters chew their toenails?

— **47** —

Why don't some people get somewhere and sit down?

— **48** —

Why don't they make Braille alphabet soup?

— **49** —

Why don't men have to wear high heels? They make them.

— **50** —

Why is "Charlie" short for "Charles" if they are both the same number of letters?

— **51** —

Why is 'abbreviation' such a long word?

— **52** —

Why is it three people can only keep a secret if two of them are dead?

— 53 —

Why is a square meal served on round plates?

— 54 —

Why is an electrical outlet called an outlet when you plug things into it? Shouldn't it be called an inlet.

— 55 —

Why is brassiere singular and panties plural?

— 56 —

Why is chopsticks one of the easiest songs to play on the piano, but the hardest thing to eat with?

— 57 —

Why is clear considered a color?

— 58 —

Why is common sense so rare?

— **59** —

Why is Friday 13th considered unlucky?

— **60** —

Why is Grape Nuts cereal called that, when it contains neither grapes, nor nuts?

— **61** —

Why is it you always run into the very person you try to avoid?

— **62** —

Why is it a 2 door car has four wheels?

— **63** —

Why is it alcoholics make better sense when they're drunk?

— **64** —

Why is it called tourist season if we can't shoot at them?

— 65 —

Why is it called a "building" when it is already built?

— 66 —

Why is it called a "drive through" if you have to stop?

— 67 —

Why is it called a soap opera when nobody sings?

— 68 —

Why is it called a TV set when there is only one?

— 69 —

Why is it called lipstick if you can still move your lips?

— 70 —

Why is it all shortcuts are too long?

— 71 —

Why is it cops don't wear light colored clothing while directing traffic at night?

— 72 —

Why is it dancing looks silly without the music?

— 73 —

Why is it everybody wants beautiful teeth but everybody hates going to the dentist?

— 74 —

Why is it everybody works so hard at having a good Christmas until they can't?

— 75 —

Why is it folks at home call you at work looking for the remote control?

— 76 —

Why is it hairdressers seem to have such bad haircuts?

— 77 —

Why is it harder to do dishes now that we have dishwashers?

— 78 —

Why is it incompetent people seem to always manage to steal the show?

— 79 —

Why is it manicurists don't get their nails done professionally?

— 80 —

Why is it manicurists' nails always look so bad?

— 81 —

Why is it men design women's bras, clothes and shoes?

— **82** —

Why is it no matter how many Chinese dishes you order, they only give you one napkin?

— **83** —

Why is it no matter what time you check into a hotel, checkout time is still the same?

— **84** —

Why do 'a fat chance' and 'a slim chance' mean the same thing?

— **85** —

Why is it nobody (even if not in a hurry) wants another car to pass them during rush hour?

— **86** —

Why is it nobody ever cleans around the base of vending machines?

— 87 —

Why is it nobody gets fired and nothing's ever done in the government ?

— 88 —

Why is it our eyes get bigger than our stomachs when we get hungry?

— 89 —

Why do you call it an asteroid when its outside the hemisphere, but call it hemorrhoid when it's in your other asteroid (posteria)?

— 90 —

Why is it that we move forward, not backward, in time?

— 94 —

Why is it some ice is slippery but not other ice?

— 92 —

If sweets are bad for us, why aren't they regulated out by the FDA?

— 93 —

Why is it the older you get the worse your memory?

— 94 —

Why is it no one wants to break silence on the elevator?

— 95 —

Why is it people deliberately sniff pepper and try not to sneeze?

— 96 —

Why is it people put death wish activities on the bucket list?

— 97 —

Why is it we invite people we don't like into our lives?

— 98 —

Why is it *stuff's* cheaper online *compared* to in the stores?

— 99 —

Why is it that as soon as you get your computer figured out, it's time for a new one?

— 100 —

Why is it the subway escalators always break when you're carrying an extra load?

— 101 —

Why is it we ask people hypothetical questions?

— 102 —

Why is it clutter doesn't bother kids as much as adults?

— 103 —

Why is it we overvalue stuff?

— **104** —

Why is stuff so hard to get rid of?

— **105** —

Why is it we allow stuff to control us?

— **106** —

Why is it Santa smells funny?

— **107** —

Why is it so easy to accumulate useless stuff?

— **108** —

Why is it so easy for a tornado to make us realize how useless our stuff is?

— **109** —

Why is it we still keep stuff around long after it has become a burden?

— **110** —

Why is it we have rooms full of stuff that is too good to use?

— 111 —

Why is it so hard to let go of stuff?

— 112 —

Why is worthless stuff so expensive?

— 113 —

Why is it bad stuff is easier to believe?

— 114 —

Why is it we remember insults more readily than compliments?

— 115 —

Why is it we attach more weight or credibility to negative things people say?

— 116 —

Why is it we keep promising ourselves we will do things that we have no intention of ever doing?

— 117 —

Why is it getting rid of junk feels so good?

— 118 —

Why is it we pack too much when we travel?

— 119 —

Why is it we hang onto stuff we don't really need?

— 120 —

Why is it our lives are crowded with things we might need one day?

— 121 —

Why is it we hang on to negative criticism?

OTHER

Part 3

Mail Call

— 1 —

Why is it people always look for someone else to blame?

— 2 —

Why is it people say they're going to "run somewhere" when they're actually going to drive?

— 3 —

Why is it people stand in line for 24 hours waiting to buy a box office ticket for a sold out show?

— 4 —

Why is it people think you're crazy when they see you talking to yourself?

— 5 —

Why is it people think it's funny to see a drunk man staggering?

— 6 —

Why is it people think stare-downs are a test of character?

— 7 —

Why is it people think they are entitled to swipe towels or other objects as keepsakes when they check out of a hotel?

— 8 —

Why is it people who can dish it out can't take it?

— 9 —

Why is it people who interrupt hate to be interrupted?

— 10 —

Why is it people who lose control of their own lives try to control other people's lives?

— **11** —

Why is it people who wear glasses can't hear until they put on their glasses?

— **12** —

Why is it people won't admit they passed gas?

— **13** —

Why is it regular people drink to make people seem interesting; but alcoholics drink because people are interesting.

— **14** —

Why is it so difficult to keep a fool from being a fool?

— **15** —

Why is it so hard to find a parking space when you're in a rush?

— **16** —

Why is it so hard to pull just one eyelash?

— 17 —

Why is it so much harder to keep a straight face when you have a legitimate reason for telling a lie?

— 18 —

Why is it some people are always running late? Why can't they just be late?

— 19 —

Why is it some people constantly make promises they cannot keep?

— 20 —

Why is it some people don't know how to shut up?

— 21 —

Why is it some people think they drive better after drinking?

— 22 —

Why is it some people think working themselves to death will get them sympathy?

— 23 —

Why is it some people won't buy insurance until they have an accident?

— 24 —

Why is it some people won't do the right thing until they're threatened?

— 25 —

Why is it taller people look down on smaller people yet smaller people still look up to them?

— 26 —

Why is it taxi drivers never look you in the eye?

— 27 —

Why is it telephone solicitors always call when it's inconvenient?

— 28 —

Why is it that depending on which way your lips are turned, happiness comes to you or runs from you?

— 29 —

Why is it that night falls but day breaks?

— 30 —

Why is it that onions and garlic stink so bad but taste so good?

— 31 —

Why is it that rain drops but snow falls?

— 32 —

Why is it that when things get wet they get darker, even though water is clear?

— 33 —

Why is it that when you transport something by car, it's called a shipment, but if by ship, it's cargo?

— 34 —

Why is it that when you're driving and looking for an address, you turn down the volume of the radio?

— 35 —

Why is it the bathroom lines are short until you have to go?

— 36 —

Why is it the bigger the house, the more junk and less room you have?

— 37 —

Why is it the congestion gets worse when cops direct traffic?

— **38** —

Why is it the dentists always seem so nice until they take a look inside your mouth?

— **39** —

Why is it the first thing psychics ask is your name? Aren't they supposed to know?

— **40** —

Why is it the floor in the repair shop's waiting area dirtier than the floors in their garages?

— **41** —

Why is it the house looks OK until you find out you have visitors coming?

— **42** —

Why is it the larger shopping malls don't post mile indicator signs?

— 43 —

Why is it the lines are always long?

— 44 —

Why is it the messages on the backs of postcards are so meaningless?

— 45 —

Why is it the newspaper is not treated like the gossip column it is?

— 46 —

Why is it the once-in-a-lifetime pictures never come out right?

— 47 —

Why is it the one time you don't bring a carry-on is the one time your luggage doesn't show up?

— 48 —

Why is it the person you're waiting on to call never calls?

— 49 —

Why is it the rain starts pouring down right at rush hour?

— 50 —

Why is it the robbers have big guns, but cops have little ones?

— 51 —

Why is it the same hike at night is shorter by day?

— 52 —

Why is it the same special deal you got was the same dealer's special that everybody else got?

— 53 —

Why is it the smallest people have the biggest mouths?

— 54 —

Why is it the very neighbor you dread contact with likes to invade your space?

— 55 —

Why is it the very people who volunteer to give presentations are so boring?

— 56 —

Why is it there are no centralized information centers with representatives from each terminal at the airport?

— 57 —

Why is it there is only one bathroom on airplanes for over two hundred people?

— 58 —

Why is it they have moving stairs and walkways at airports but they don't have moving car-ways?

— 59 —

Why is it they put huge gas trucks out on the highway?

— 60 —

Why is it vendors keep selling irregular panty hose to people?

— 61 —

Why is it we call it a creamer if it's non-dairy?

— 62 —

Why is it we call it a day at night?

— 63 —

Why is it we call it an original copy?

— 64 —

Why is it we complain about fast food places but we keep going back?

— 65 —

Why is it we expect waitresses to keep smiling?

— 66 —

Why is it we give so much power and control to a computer?

— 67 —

Why is it we need to clone ourselves?

— 68 —

Why is it we never notice when somebody's wearing new eyeglasses?

— 69 —

Why is it we offer junk we don't want to our best friends?

— 70 —

Why is it we pass everyone else in traffic just to get caught by the next traffic light in the very next block?

— 71 —

Why is it we trust computers more than programmers?

— 72 —

Why is it we're trying to make the body go one hundred times faster than it was designed? Why are we in such a hurry?

— 73 —

Why is it when people say "don't look now" we do?

— 74 —

Why is it we can still live after being scared to death?

— 75 —

Why is it when you attempt to pass a slow driver in the fast lane, he speeds up just enough to block you from going around the car directly in front of you?

— 76 —

Why is it you can eat at twenty different places and all of the French fried potatoes taste different?

— 77 —

Why is the 0 on a phone after 1 and not before 1?

— 78 —

Why is the third hand on the watch called a second hand?

— 79 —

Why is the word dictionary in the dictionary?

— 80 —

Why is there a light in the fridge and not in the freezer?

— 81 —

Why is there a top line on lined paper if we never use it?

— 82 —

Why is there always one in every crowd?

— 83 —

Why is there no "w" in "one", but there is a "w" in "two" and we don't use it?

— 84 —

Why is vanilla extract is brown but vanilla ice cream is white?

— 85 —

Why isn't phonetic spelled the way it sounds?

— 86 —

Why isn't chocolate considered a vegetable, since it comes from cocoa beans?

— 87 —

Will plants still grow if you yell instead of talking to them?

— 88 —

Why can't we simply press 'Ctrl Alt Delete' and start all over when we mess up?

— 89 —

Wouldn't it be smart to make the sticky stuff on envelopes taste like chocolate?

— 90 —

Why do we always get a red light when in a hurry?

— 91 —

Why must one have to go through trials to get patience?

— 92 —

Why is it a single hair on your chin irks you more than those growing anywhere else?

— 93 —

Why is it that going down sweet memory lane isn't all that sweet?

— 94 —

Why it is the more goodies we enjoy, the more we want?!

Citations / Resources

Quotes cited selected from *www.goodreads.com/* and *www.brainyquote.com/*

Pg 9, Nelson Mandela, "There is no passion to be found playing small... "
Pg 12, John C. Maxwell, "The greatest day in your life and mine...."
Pg 30, Soren Kierkegaard, "Life is not a problem to be solved..."
Pg 82, Leo Buscaglia, "Too often we underestimate the power of ...."
Pg 149, Voltaire, "God gave us the gift of life..."

Made in the USA
Middletown, DE
20 February 2018